THE AESTHETIC COMPASS

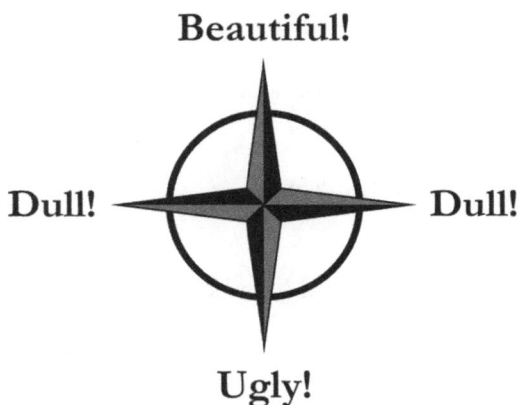

Beautiful!

Dull! — Dull!

Ugly!

Foundation of Leadership Action and Inaction

BOB EMILIANI, PH.D.

Foreword by Ken Eakin

The Aesthetic Compass: Foundation of Leadership Action and Inaction / Bob Emiliani

Cover design by Bob Emiliani

ISBN-13: 978-1-7320191-5-7
Library of Congress Control Number: 2022905173

1. Aesthetics 2. Leadership 3. Management 4. Business
5. Economics 6. Sociology 7. Philosophy

First Edition: April 2022

Published by Cubic LLC, South Kingstown, Rhode Island, USA.

This publication is believed to provide accurate information with respect to the subject matter covered. It is sold with the understanding that it does not in any way represent legal, financial, business, consulting, or other professional service.

Manufactured using digital print-on-demand technology.

CONTENTS

"The more things change, the more they stay the same."

- Jean-Baptiste Alphonse Karr

Foreword

Imagine your own workplace. Think of how the tables and chairs in the break room are arranged. What materials are they made of? Do they have a pleasing shape, feel, and color? What about the floor, the walls, the windows, the lighting, the ceiling? What do you hear, smell, taste? Now consider the way different people at your workplace dress, the cars they drive, the way they sound or smell. What do the work environments they inhabit (cubicles, shop floor, corner office, etc.) signify? What about various people's behaviors, their choice of words, their tone of voice, their eye-contact, their bodily posture and gestures? What about the graphs and charts used in your business' dashboards, the PowerPoint presentations, or the annual reports? Have you ever considered any of these things to be ugly or beautiful or dull?

Perhaps you are confused. The word "aesthetic" is not often associated with work, business, or management. To the average person, aesthetics has to do with definitions of beauty in relation to the fine arts like painting, sculpture, architecture, theatre, music, opera, and dance. Classical aesthetics seeks to define what makes fine art "great" or not. It is judgmental. It is elitist. It is about taste and values. It is about cultivating the sensibility to distinguish between what is "universally" beautiful and ugly. This does not sound like anything Bob Emiliani would write about.

Contemporary aesthetics has moved away from claiming to be able to make objective, categorical judgements about art. It eschews any notions of universal beauty, recognizing that perceptions of beauty are very much relative to the beholder's culture and background. Given this relativism, contemporary aesthetics focuses on experiences and feelings over judgments and values. It also widens its field of vision to consider the experiences created by non-art objects and what has been traditionally considered popular or "low" art, such as film, television, advertising, illustration, and design. But contemporary aesthetics has not, until now, contemplated management.

In *The Aesthetic Compass*, Emiliani uses the term "aesthetics" in both a classical and contemporary sense. He speaks of aesthetic *experiences* (perceptions and emotions) and aesthetic *judgements* (cognition). He places his focus squarely on non-art objects and behaviors: specifically, those of leadership and management. What *The Aesthetic Compass* makes clear is that the nexus between management and aesthetics resides, in the fundamental nature of human perception, emotion, and cognition.

When you look at a painting for the first time, it creates some degree of emotional reaction in you before you do much thinking about it. It goes from your eyes straight to the emotional centers of the brain, and, potentially, if it carries enough emotional weight, other areas of your body. It does not involve your higher brain functions much at all. Your emotional reaction might be one of transcendence and awe or it could be one of shock and disgust. Often, it is neither. The art may not affect you strongly one way or the other. It is just neutral or boring. The point is that the painting affects your bodily sensations and emotions *before* it engages your thinking and judgement. We use only a modicum of mental energy to make the semantic distinctions of "beautiful," "ugly," or "dull" *retroactively* to our experience. Our thinking certainly can amplify or dampen our feelings, but it is important to note, and contrary to popular opinion, that we sense and feel the world *before* we think about it.

Deep thinking is hard. It is unpleasant. We tend to avoid it. As the work of Daniel Kahneman and other cognitive psychologists have illustrated, we are mentally lazy. Consequently, we are pretty good at labeling and categorizing our sensory experiences to avoid thinking hard, especially about unpleasant things. We use mental models, also known as "schemata" or "heuristics" in cognitive science, that allow us to economize our mental energy. Our brains quickly slot the sensory stimuli from new situations into familiar, prefabricated categories. This makes the strange seem familiar, the unusual seem common, and the novel seem like it is old hat. It is a mental habit that is comforting to us. Therefore, when we perceive art for the first time, we tend to quickly categorize it as either "beautiful" or "ugly" or "dull" in our minds and do not think about it anymore – at least not if it falls into the ugly or dull categories.

It may now be easier to see how perception, emotion, and cognition play a role in management and particularly in management decision-making. If you are, say, a senior leader evaluating new proposals put forth by subordinates for a new business venture, you will first react *emotionally* to the proposals, as if they were paintings, and this emotion will trigger a mental schema that enables you to make quick decisions about whether the proposals are "beautiful," "ugly," or "dull". The "good/bad proposal" schema makes light work of your decision-making, relieving your higher cognitive brain functions of much effort. In other words, you will first have an *aesthetic experience*, involving your perceptions and emotions, which then leads you to make a quick *aesthetic judgement*, your cognitive response to the emotion. This aesthetic model of decision-making goes against the mainstream assumption found in business schools and the popular media: that management is largely governed by frontal brain lobe rationality, untainted by base emotions more typically displayed by those occupying lower ranks in the hierarchy.

Where do our mental schemata come from? No doubt some of our schemata are built "bottom up" based on learning from positive and negative sensory-emotional experiences we have as children. But most of our mental schemata, as adults, come to us "top down," as we become more and more aware of what emotions, behaviors and opinions that are considered acceptable, desirable, or taboo in certain social contexts, including business contexts. In other words, schemata are provided by the culture and social norms that precede our engagement with new situations.

If we are in a new situation, we may not know what to feel, do, or say, so we look around at what others are doing in the same or similar situations and take our cues from them. When we don't have an internal point of reference, when we lack a helpful schema through which we can make sense of what we are experiencing, we feel awkward and uncomfortable. Think of your first kiss, or perhaps when you were travelling in a foreign culture and were not aware of local customs. Once we have acquired some experience in kissing or navigating a foreign culture (or, perhaps, with some luck, kissing foreigners!), we have acquired mental schemata that help us mitigate or avoid these unpleasant feelings in the future. In this way, schemata have a functional utility. They direct our attention and behavior towards what we have learned is "beautiful," helping us experience more positive emotional states. They also reject, ignore, or suppress what we have determined is "ugly," helping us avoid negative emotional states. These schemata are useful navigational aids in our emotional self-preservation.

Analogously, when an individual becomes a leader of others for the first time, or when a leader is promoted to a position of higher authority, it is, despite some obvious perks, a strange, novel, and uncomfortable situation. Flooded with new sensory information and the unpleasant feelings of awkwardness that accompany it, the mind seeks to make sense of it all. Unconsciously, we rely on the pre-existing, centuries-old norms of leadership behavior to provide a schema for "how to behave like a leader" in the present. Thus, the present imitates the past, and the status quo of leadership tends to perpetuate itself.

The Aesthetic Compass elucidates how cultural norms of management behaviors have remained largely unchanged since at least the days of the industrial revolution. This dominant, inherited tradition of management behaviors is what Emiliani calls "classical management." It is reinforced on all sides by the social, economic, political, historical, philosophical, educational, technological, cultural, spiritual, legal, and, yes, *aesthetic* traditions that hold sway within organizations and society, forming a nearly impregnable fortress of management schemata – commonly referred to as values and beliefs – that drive decision-making and behavior.

Allowing into consciousness new information that might cause us to question our existing schemata would make us vulnerable again to feelings of uncertainty, chaos, confusion, and awkwardness. Thus, our natural tendency is to keep new information, like barbarian invaders, outside our castle walls by either assimilating only the "beautiful" information or, more likely, dismissing and rejecting it altogether as simply "ugly" and not worthy of our attention. Once formed, schemata tend only to be reinforced over time and become very hard to modify or displace in our minds.

Given these workings of human perception, emotion, and cognition, it is hardly surprising that when managers at all levels are presented with an objectively superior – but dramatically *different* – system of management, it is rejected on purely aesthetic grounds. It is not given any serious, rational consideration. There is no weighing of factual evidence, nor any careful analysis of the pros and cons. That would be far too cognitively demanding and emotionally threatening because "progressive management," as Emiliani calls it, stirs up all sorts of unpleasant fears of loss in leaders: the loss of rights and privileges, honor, wealth, power, and influence. Thus, progressive management is usually rejected immediately as "ugly." It is a bodily, "gut" decision, made by executives much like the way one might decide that a Jackson Pollock drip painting is "ugly."

The original and important contribution that *The Aesthetic Compass* makes to the study of management is that Emiliani brings the body – the messy, dirty, chaotic world of bodily sensations and emotions – into his provocative and incisive analysis of why classical management repeatedly rejects the many forms of progressive management.

Emiliani is a staunch advocate for a better system of management but feels that until we understand the current realities of executive thinking, we have little hope of bringing about positive change on a more widespread basis. To better understand current executive thinking, he argues, we cannot continue to look through the traditional lens of rationality. We must instead look through an aesthetic lens to understand the immense power that the perceptual-emotional realm has in maintaining the ironclad values and beliefs of classical management.

Ken Eakin
April 2022
Ottawa, Ontario

Preface

This book represents the endpoint of a line of work that I began more than 15 years ago. Simply put, it is to understand why, as Jean-Baptiste Karr said more than 150 years ago, "The more things change, the more they stay the same" [1]. The context of Karr's words, for this book, is how organizations are led and managed. Specifically, why are organizations led and managed in mostly the same ways today as described in books written in the 17th, 18th, and 19th centuries? What accounts for the durability of such ways of thinking and doing things given that so much has else changed over the centuries?

I have devoted thirty years of my life to advancing progressive forms of leadership and management. I, as well as most others, have invariably encountered overwhelming disinterest among top leaders for the many and deep changes that are needed to replace classical management with progressive management [2-3]. My advocacy for progressive management is rooted in personal experience. Of all my years of professional work in organizations, it is effortless to say that my best experiences, by far, where those years where the organization was led by a leader who embraced progressive management; someone who was not bound by outdated traditions and who recognized that satisfying the wants and needs of employees, customers and other stakeholders required improved ways of leading and managing the enterprise. The old ways were too heavy a burden for the leader that had to be shed.

My advocacy for progressive management is also based on the view that meliorative trends are not automatic consequences of human thinking and action. To think otherwise is to be bound to preconceptions that prevent critical analysis of problems. In fact, stagnation, and more likely regression, are inevitable in the long run in the absence of clear-eyed curiosity to understand cause-and-effect and rapidly improve deteriorating conditions. Such an action orientation is made possible by replacing archaic preconceptions with human sensory perceptions.

A management system that is oriented towards favoring change, improvement, and making progress as times change – keeping up with the times [4-6] – is far more difficult to establish than one would imagine. What stands in the way? The complex, interlocking network of barriers that retard progress have been fully deconstructed in previous works [7-9]. But can this complex story be simplified? The aim of this book is to offer an Occam's razor explanation for the largely static way in which organizations have been led and managed by generations of leaders. Occam's razor is stated as [10-11]:

"plurality should not be posited without necessity"

or

"entities should not be multiplied beyond necessity"

and generally interpreted as a principle expressing the preference for simpler theories because they can be tested more easily than complex competing theories [12]. That does not exclude complex theories from explaining the phenomenon under consideration. In popular culture,

Occam's razor is stated inaccurately as "the simplest explanation is usually the best one." So, in the present volume, a simpler theory is presented to explain a phenomenon whose underlying workings are complex [7-9, 13] and consistent with available empirical data.

A previous work briefly examined how aesthetic judgments contribute to making leaders captive to the status quo of classical management [8]. But upon deeper analysis, aesthetic judgements do much more than just "contribute." *The Aesthetic Compass* was written to make the case that aesthetics are more powerful than is realized when it comes to the processing of information in relation to the job of leading and managing organizations [14]. Aesthetics may even be, in most cases, the fundamental determinant of action or inaction that limits how far leaders will move beyond the status quo. Said another way, aesthetics plays an integral role in decision-making, one that assures continuity with past ways of thinking and doing things. Aesthetic judgments rely on preconceptions to validate what is beautiful and what is ugly, and both aesthetic judgments and preconceptions are absorbed through social learning that is seamlessly passed on from one generation of leaders to the next. As such, aesthetics acts as a compass that provides seemingly clear and accurate direction to leaders that points toward beauty.

This book aims to avoid making value-based judgments. Instead, the desire is to present the "lay of the land" so that readers can consider what improvements they need to make in how they lead and manage organizations. At times the writing may seem like criticism of leaders. That is not the intent, for the author recognizes that if he were in the shoes of a top leader, he would likely think and do the same as they do. In places where value judgment or criticism has creeped in, I ask for your forgiveness and hope that it does not detract from the central arguments put forth in this volume.

This is the 25th book that I have authored or co-authored. Writing reflects not just a labor that I have loved doing for over 40 years, but it also reflects a deeply sincere effort on my part to help people see realities and make improvements that benefit themselves, their team, their organization, its stakeholders, and humanity. In my practical research and writing, I have always strived to thoughtfully present new and unique points of view, information, and methods that motivated individuals can put into practice. Otherwise, what is the point of doing such work if it is not new and unique?

My hope is that readers will recognize the practical nature of this work [15], contemplate the importance of aesthetics in determining leadership action and inaction, and find ways to advance the very important practice of leadership and management of organizations; to move past classical management, having served its purpose but now obsolete in most ways, and enter a progressive realm of leadership and management that better reflects the times people live in.

Bob Emiliani
Wakefield, Rhode Island
April 2022

Notes

[1] This epigram is attributed to Jean-Baptiste Alphonse Karr circa 1848: *"Plus ça change, plus c'est la même chose."* https://en.wikipedia.org/wiki/Jean-Baptiste_Alphonse _Karr, accessed 18 February 2022

[2] "Classical management" is a descriptive term for traditional systems and methods used to lead and manage organizations, the origins of which date to 350 years ago, and longer, wherein little or no effort is made by top leaders to question if specific traditions are outdated and no longer useful. If such questioning were to occur, it would give way to progressive forms of leadership and management. Such questioning rarely occurs because classical management is rooted in preconceptions. "Progressive management" is a descriptive term for modern systems and methods used to lead and manage organizations, wherein top leaders frequently question whether specific traditions remain useful. If not, they are discarded and replaced with the aim of keeping up with changing times and making progress. Progressive management is not without its own traditions, but clear distinctions are made between traditions that seem timeless and those that clearly are not. In progressive management, traditions pertain to the obligation for affecting change and evolution, while in classical management traditions pertain to the obligation for maintaining the status quo. An important difference between the two is the mindset: "Try it and see what happens" (progressive) versus "It works, don't change" (classical).

[3] The earliest form of modern progressive management was Scientific Management, created by Frederick Winslow Taylor and his many colleagues in the period from about 1880-1930, most of whom were mechanical engineers. Scientific management led to the creation of Industrial Engineering, upon which Toyota's management system was built starting in 1937 and has continuously evolved since then. In 1988, Toyota's innovative management system led to a Western derivative interpretation first named "lean production" and later named "Lean management." These two current forms of modern progressive management are rooted in scientific thinking (cause-and-effect; observation, hypothesis, experimentation, analysis, conclusion [repeat]) and the engineering mindset of trial and error. Under this mainly objective construct, the focus is on system and process, and these as the source of problems (not people), and so the ability to make timely progress in leadership and management practice is obvious. In contrast, classical management has ancient origins, and its precepts and practices are rooted in privilege and preconceptions. Under this mainly subjective experiential and intuitive construct, the focus is on people and thus deliberate avoidance of rationality. People are the problem, not system and process, so better leadership and management lags the need for change by decades or more.

[4] The image below depicts the origin and evolution of classical management and progressive management. Classical management, being rooted in privilege and preconceptions, is largely unchanged over time. Progressive management, being rooted in sensory perceptions informed by scientific thinking (scientific method, causality) and trial and error,

evolves over time. As the image makes clear, these are two dramatically different systems of leadership and management thinking and practice. Timelines not to scale.

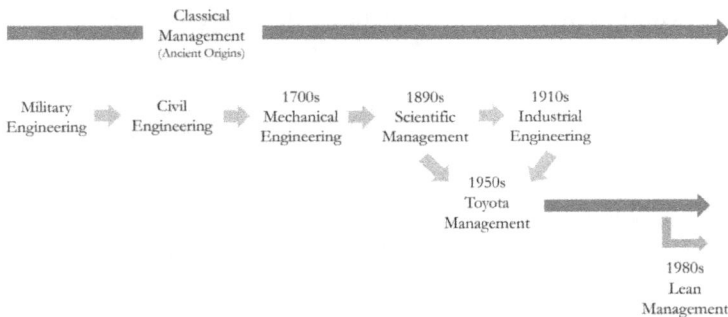

[5] The early major works of Scientific Management, later evolving into the technical discipline of industrial Engineering, include: Taylor, F.W. (1911), *Principles of Scientific Management*, Harper and Brothers, New York, New York • Cooke, M. (1913), "The Spirit and Social Significance of Scientific Management," *The Journal of Political Economy*, Vol. 21, No. 6, June, pp. 481-493 • Gilbreth, F.B. (1914), *Primer of Scientific Management*, D. Van Nostrand Co., New York, New York • Gilbreth, L.M. (1914), *The Psychology of Management*, Sturgis and Walton Co., New York, New York • Taylor, F. W. (1947), "Taylor's Testimony Before the Special House Committee" in *Scientific Management: Comprising Shop Management, Scientific Management, Testimony Before the Special House Committee*, Foreword by H. S. Person, Harper and Row Publishers, New York, New York ("Testimony of Mr. Frederick Winslow Taylor," *Hearings Before Special Committee of the House of Representatives to Investigate the Taylor and Other Systems of Shop Management Under Authority of H. Res. 90,*

Volume 3, 25 January 1912, pp. 1377-1508)

[6] Modern progressive management takes the general form of the management system developed by Toyota Motor Corporation. Major works include: Monden, Y. (1983), *Toyota Production System: Practical Approach to Production Management*, First Edition, Engineering and Management Press, Norcross, Georgia • Lu, D. (1985), *Kanban: Just-In-Time at Toyota*, Productivity Press, Portland, Oregon, 1985 • Ohno, T. (1988), *Toyota Production System – Beyond Large-Scale Production*, Productivity Press, Portland, Oregon • Ohno, T. (1988), *Workplace Management*, Productivity Press, Cambridge, Massachusetts • Ohno, T. and Mito, S. (1988), *Just-In-Time For Today and Tomorrow*, Productivity Press, Cambridge, Massachusetts • Shinohara, I. (1988), *NPS New Production System: JIT Crossing Industry Boundaries*, Productivity Press, Cambridge, Massachusetts • Liker, J. (2004), *The Toyota Way*, McGraw-Hill, New York, New York • Kato, I. and Smalley, A. (2011), *Toyota Kaizen Methods: Six Steps to Improvement*, CRC Press, Boca Raton, Florida

[7] Emiliani, B. (2018), *The Triumph of Classical Management Over Lean Management: How Tradition Prevails and What to Do About It*, Cubic LLC, South Kingstown, Rhode Island

[8] Emiliani, B. (2020), *Irrational Institutions: Business, Its Leaders, and The Lean Movement*, Cubic LLC, South Kingstown, Rhode Island

[9] Emiliani, B. (2020), *Management Mysterium: The Quest for Progress*, Cubic LLC, South Kingstown, Rhode Island

[10] See https://en.wikipedia.org/wiki/William_of_Ockh am, accessed 18 February 2022

[11] See https://www.britannica.com/topic/Occams-razor, https://en.wikipedia.org/wiki/Occam%27s_razor, https://www.aaas.org/origin-and-popular-use-occams-razor, and http://www.philosophical-investigations.org/2018/05/occa ms-razor-on-virtue-of-simplicity.html, accessed 18 February 2022

[12] Readers should never understand "theory" as something that is abstract, impractical, speculative, or irrelevant in the "real world." This is a mistake that many people make in the popularized use of the word. A theory is a proposed explanation whose validity is determined by conducting experiments. Upon testing, the theory may be found to be a valid, one that is useful for making predictions, and become regarded as fact. Its predictive capability may one day be surpassed by a new theory which is then subjected to experiments to determine its validity.

[13] The positing and evaluation of a simpler theory explaining the static way in which most organizations have been led and managed by generations of leaders is made using empirical data from varied "real world" sources. These include observations of experiments performed daily in organizations, better known as executive decision-making. As such, the analyses contained in this book are grounded in the reality of the everyday work of leaders.

[14] In this book, leadership and management are understood to be of the form yin and yang, the Chinese philosophy of dualism, where seemingly contradictory or different forces are complementary to one another and thus interconnected or interrelated to one another. The image below represents leadership as yang (white) and management as yin (black). Within each there are seeds of the other (black and white circles inscribed with letters M and L). Thus, leadership does exist without management and vice versa.

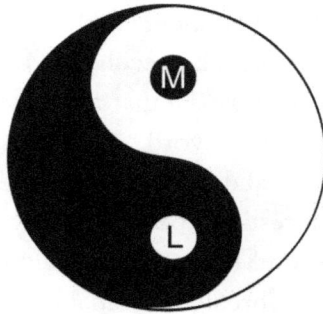

This contrasts with the usual representation where leadership and management are seen as being distinctly different and lacking in complementarity (see Abraham Zaleznik, "Managers and Leaders: Are They Different?, *Harvard Business Review*, May-June 1977). Additionally, the use of the terms "leader," "leaders," and "leadership" in this book should be understood to mean individual leaders (principally, but not exclusive to, CEO, president, vice president) as well as leadership teams (i.e., the officers of the company or organization). Where such distinction is unclear, readers can infer one or both as the context dictates.

[15] This volume, as well as the three preceding volumes (see Notes 7-9) are, in essence, critiques of the current state of leadership and management. As such, these highly detailed analyses and candid assessments point the way to improvement.

Introduction

"When everyone knows beauty is beauty, this is ugly."
                                        - Lao Tzu

The replacement of classical management with progressive management and associated leadership routines has proven, over a span of more than 120 years, to be remarkably difficult. It is no exaggeration to say that tens of thousands of people have tried and failed to convince top leaders there are much better ways of thinking and doing things than classical management. Many have lost their job or have been sidelined for trying. We find that factual evidence does not persuade most leaders to abandon classical management. Immense stacks of practitioner-focused books and academic research papers, filled with exhaustive facts, logical arguments, financial data, non-financial data, survey data, testimonials, and so on, do not persuade [1]. Neither do visits to exemplary organizations nor exhortations from fellow leaders who have successfully replaced classical management with progressive management [2]. Not even hype sells progressive management. These empirical results confirm that something much deeper is going on, the details of which have only recently been described [3].

Remarkably, the negative reaction that top leaders have to progressive management is formed very quickly, often within minutes. Their judgment seems almost instinctive, preceding thought, which suggests that the limbic part of the brain (emotional or feeling) and the brain stem (reptilian or instinct) are activated. Once formed, the negative reaction to progressive management it is nearly impossible to correct. Leaders either like it or they don't, and few change their opinion. If such a reaction is activated by these primal parts of the brain, it suggests that emotions and self-preservation play a key role in judging the merits of progressive management. And that's where aesthetics and aesthetic judgments come into play because they too are informed by the primitive parts of the human brain. Aesthetics may then be an Occam's razor explanation for the static ways in which hierarchical organizations are led and managed.

Absent the insights that come from aesthetics or deeper analyses and understanding of complex phenomena [3], the study and practice of leadership and management is focused on what is most easily observable: traits, skills, personality, behaviors, emotions, and the like, generally with great emphasis on "me," the leader, rather than "them," the followers. This leader-centered emphasis is apparent in books and training by the extensive guidance given on what to do, rather than clear explications of what followers dislike from their leaders; what not to do. Furthermore, the common prescriptions for becoming a capable leader fail to identify in detail the hundreds of possible basic errors that leaders make which, if avoided, would quickly result in better leadership and management of organizations [4].

The role of aesthetics in the leadership and management of organizations [5] is an underdeveloped area of study principally because it is not recognized as being important. Aesthetics is assumed to be either irrelevant or somehow embedded, inconsequentially, in other phenomena such that it is not worthy of stand-alone consideration. This book hopes to change that uninformed perspective by showing how aesthetics plays a major role in leadership and management design and their day-to-day functioning, whether outcomes are successful or not. By bringing aesthetics to the forefront, readers will gain an appreciation for how this intangible yet strongly felt sensory perception (including bodily comfort or discomfort) affects everyone in an organization as well as external stakeholders.

The objective of this book is to interpret leadership and management through the lens of aesthetics – aesthetic experiences and aesthetic judgments – with the goal of improving how organizations are led and managed. This is in recognition of the fact that organizations today are led much the same way as they have been led in the past. Absent technology, the human interaction and related aesthetic inputs to those interactions have remained relatively constant over time. How long? Perhaps for as long as organizations of people with identifiable purpose have existed, or perhaps for as short as the past 500 years. Regardless, there are fundamentals of human interaction in organizations that are guided by aesthetic imperatives hidden from sight. The hope is to take aesthetic qualities that are normally hidden and make them visible for all to see. In that way, we can better understand leadership action and inaction, as well as pathways for improvement.

Aesthetics is not something that people typically think about outside the domains of art and architecture [6]. Its existence in other realms is neglected because we easily look past it or think it is irrelevant. This is true of aesthetics and the aesthetic experiences in the workplace, as they lack the special way in which art-centered aesthetic experiences move people. While the built environment that people work in everyday certainly has noticeable aesthetic qualities – beautiful, ugly, dull, or nondescript – what is less noticeable is the role of aesthetics in shared everyday experiences resulting from human interaction in hierarchical workplaces.

What is aesthetics [7]?

> "The word aesthetic is derived from the Greek αἰσθητικός – aisthetikos, meaning 'aesthetic, sensitive, sentient, **pertaining to sense perception**'...
>
> ...a branch of philosophy that deals with **the nature of beauty and taste**... It examines **aesthetic values** often expressed through **judgments of taste**...
>
> It considers what happens in our minds when we engage with aesthetic objects or environments such as viewing visual art, listening to music, reading poetry, **experiencing a play**, or exploring nature.
>
> ...Aesthetics considers why people like some works of art and not others, as well as **how art can affect moods or even our beliefs**.

In the above description, bold has been added to key phrases to highlight the subjective nature of aesthetics. It is a matter of one's personal experience and thus personal taste. Beauty is in the eye of the beholder, as this ancient saying goes. Ugly is also in the eye of the beholder. And so is the dull or ordinary. Aesthetic experience is the sensory feelings that come over us when we see, hear, touch, taste, or smell something that moves us. Those feelings lead to aesthetic judgment of beautiful or ugly, like or dislike, though sometimes resulting in an experience of indifference or dullness.

Obviously, when it comes to visual art, we each have our own judgment of what is beautiful and ugly. To many people, Johannes Vermeer's *Girl with a Pearl Earring* (c. 1665) painting is beautiful, while Jackson Pollock's *Red Composition* (1946) drip painting is ugly. They cannot be convinced *Red Composition* is a great painting or that Mr. Pollock was a great artist. They will ignore such claims and say, "I just don't like it!" It is, after all, a matter of taste. To some, the reverse is true; Pollack was brilliant and original while Vermeer was merely one of many painters doing similar types of work. Vermeer's work evokes order, harmony, simplicity, and familiarity. Pollock's work evokes disorder, chaos, complexity, and strangeness. Which do you like better?

The same is true for architecture. To some an aesthetic of the present, Modernist architecture, is beautiful. To others it is ugly. Their preference is Victorian or Arts and Crafts architecture. Which aesthetic do you prefer? Aesthetics of the past or aesthetics of the present? When we give some thought to the things we like and dislike, we discover aesthetics quickly and powerfully informs our judgments for most of the things that we interact with in our daily lives, not just art. Aesthetics is not just a philosophy of art. Aesthetics is everywhere. It is the foundation of all human experiences.

Here are examples of things we aesthetically experience:

- Painting
- Theater
- Music
- Illustration
- Books
- Movies
- Homes
- Architecture
- Doors
- Cars
- Colors
- Pens
- Tools

- Fashion
- Rugs
- Food
- Drink
- Scenery
- Flowers
- Pets
- Stores
- Scenery
- Humor
- Face
- Hair
- Body

We quickly make judgments of beauty or ugliness because our brain automatically seeks to create order and coherence to the mass of information that we are exposed to every day. Aesthetic judgments help us sort through the information, make sense of it, and determine what should hold our attention and what should bypass our attention. In short, things must look a certain way to be judged as beautiful or ugly. The judgment of beauty is socially constructed, both early and later in life. We tend to see as beautiful what most other people see as beautiful, aided by preconceptions – socially accepted aesthetics. It helps us fit into social groups more easily and avoid conflict. But, to see things differently as not so beautiful or even ugly, is to risk being shunned or expelled from the group, an ugly painful experience that most people will seek to avoid. So, they may publicly say that something is beautiful while privately thinking it is ugly.

Given the above list, why would the limbic part of the brain (emotional or feeling part) and the brain stem (reptilian or instinct) not be activated when it encounters information about leadership and management? Is it not likely that aesthetics quickly and powerfully informs leaders' judgments for most of the things that they experience at work? That, of course, includes people, departments, metrics, other organizations (e.g., suppliers), and, of course, management systems. Top leaders may think of the organization, its systems, methods, and processes, as an aesthetic, one that they have a hand in creating (e.g., startup) or are responsible for maintaining (e.g., long-established business). No art is perfect; all art has flaws yet can still be judged to be beautiful. Likewise, a management system can have flaws and still be judged as beautiful whether or not one had a hand in creating or maintaining it.

The basis for making aesthetic judgments is human sensory perceptions: sight, sound, touch, smell, and taste. We must add "gut" as the sixth sense because most leaders say it plays a significant role in executive decision-making (Figure I-1). Gut is, of course, a proxy for "emotion" or, at times, an intangible and completely unverifiable rationale for choosing to do or not do something. Leaders evaluating information will rely principally on sight, sound, and gut. They may touch documents or computer keyboards or say, "this smells bad" or "this puts a bad taste in my mouth," but sight, sound, and gut are the dominant senses used when making aesthetic judgments [8-9], of which decision-making is one form.

Related to this is "aesthetic memory." The aesthetic of times

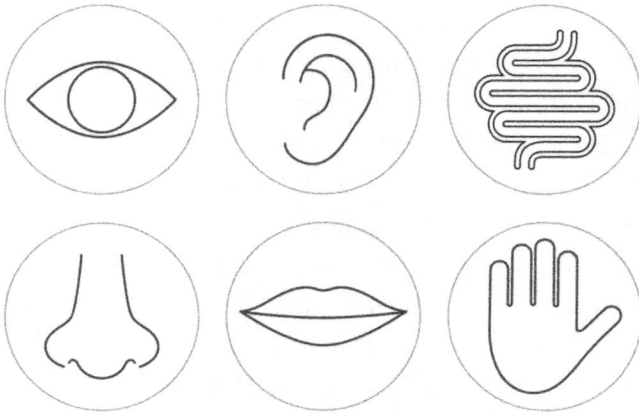

Figure I-1. Six human senses. The top row, sight, sound, and gut are central to executive thinking and decision-making. Touch (getting one's hands dirty) is the least useful sense for leaders.

past, whether lived or not. Aesthetic memory will be used by leaders to glorify new efforts to bring the past forward to the present; a desire to revive old ways of thinking and doing things because they are judged as having worked well in the past. The question becomes is revival of aesthetic memory invoked to satisfy the present wants and needs of the organization, or to satisfy the present wants and needs of those who run the enterprise? Does aesthetic memory brought forward to the present solve current organizational problems, or does it allow leaders to avoid certain problems that they personally face?

A further consideration is the durability of aesthetic judgments. When a social group makes a judgment and determines that something is either beautiful or ugly, the judgment tends to be long-lasting. In physics, a ball in motion stays in motion unless acted upon by an unbalanced force.

Similarly, aesthetic judgements of beauty can last for decades or centuries, until such time a succeeding social group makes a judgment and determines something that was once beautiful is now dull or ugly. In this way, aesthetic judgments are both long-lived and transitory, as is more clearly apparent in the fashion clothing or hairstyling industries due to the short life cycle of styles yet they remain fixed in memory.

Finally, in the context of how organizations are led and managed, aesthetics does not lie only in the physical realm of the built environment. It also lies in the intangible or invisible realm of our minds, something thought and "felt" but not necessarily seen or physically graspable. Examples of this are corporate culture and the so-called "tone" that is set by top leaders [10]. The aesthetic judgment made about such work environments can be beautiful (welcoming, supportive) or ugly (blaming, judgmental), or vary between these two conditions depending upon the leader residing at any level of the organization. A beautiful organizational culture may contain some leaders who are agents of ugly aesthetics, while an ugly organizational culture may contain some leaders who are agents of beautiful aesthetics.

The upcoming chapters describe how aesthetics objects inform leaders' aesthetic experiences and aesthetic judgments in ways that delay or halt progress in leadership and management thinking and practice. Chapter 1 describes aesthetic objects that are hidden or do not seem to generate an aesthetic experience – the everyday things that we look past and fail to appreciate due to the familiarity of our daily routines. Yet these are important contributors to overall aesthetic experiences, good or bad, and, crucially, they deeply inform leadership thinking and decision-making.

Chapter 2 examines the aesthetics of classical management. Through this lens we discover why classical management endures despite the existence of progressive management that is better suited for current and future needs. Chapter 3 explores the subject of management design from an aesthetic perspective, comparing and contrasting the aesthetics of classical management to the aesthetics of progressive management. Chapter 4 examines the nature of path dependence and lock-in, which prevents leaders from switching to a new path of progressive leadership and management practice.

It is hoped that this unique aesthetic perspective gives readers a clear understanding of why "The more things change, the more they stay the same," and leads to insights that will produce needed change. Readers are encouraged to use their imagination and think creatively to find solutions to the problems described in this volume.

Ideas for Improvement

List some ideas to improve aesthetic experiences for employees and other stakeholders. Try out your ideas.

-

-

-

-

-

-

Notes

[1] In general, personal beliefs are one's personal aesthetics. They are powerful to the point where facts may not produce a revision in beliefs. Personal aesthetics are unchanged because they serve one well from the very important standpoint of social interaction. To change one's beliefs means one may have to change social groups, which is personally uncomfortable and potentially costly to one's status and reputation. The social aesthetics that we create to please ourselves and our social group make us feel good. Through the years we creatively paint pictures in our minds of pleasing aesthetics that are difficult to undo. We are all artists of our own beliefs. Our aesthetics may be one thing in public and another thing in private, so you may never really know what other people think. Different aesthetics are created for different circumstances as the need arises: work (subordinates, peers, superiors, departments, external stakeholders), home, politics, religion, sports, food, etc.

[2] Emiliani, B. et al. (2007), *Better Thinking, Better Results: Case Study and Analysis of an Enterprise-Wide Lean Transformation*, Second Edition, The CLBM, LLC, Wethersfield, Conn.

[3] See Preface, Notes 7-9

[4] Emiliani, B. (2015), *Speed Leadership: A New Way to Lead for Rapidly Changing Times*, The CLBM, LLC Wethersfield, Connecticut

[5] This volume is principally concerned with the role of

aesthetics in the leadership and management of private organizations whose function is for-profit business. That does not exclude the role of aesthetics in the leadership and management of nonprofits, government, or other types of organizations. It will be apparent to readers that aesthetics plays an equally strong role there as well.

[6] For an interesting expansion of the understanding of aesthetics in everyday life, see Saito, Y. (2007), *Everyday Aesthetics*, Oxford University Press, New York, New York

[7] https://en.wikipedia.org/wiki/Aesthetics, accessed 22 February 2022

[8] "Gut" is part of the human somatic nervous system activated when processing information for leadership decision-making. It is hoped that leaders make decisions based on facts, supported to a lesser extent by gut (emotional feeling of comfort). This would typically be the case in progressive management. The situation is different in classical management. Often, leaders are told what they want to hear, not what they need to hear, and, consequently, are greatly deficient in the facts. The combination of being misinformed and the likely overreliance on gut – owing to the leader being in a state of comfort having been told what they want to hear – greatly increases the probability of poor decisions. This will, in turn, require resources to be expended to correct the problems that result from poor decisions – resources that could have been saved or used elsewhere if leaders are willing to hear the facts. Yet, classical management's design is such that it is important for leaders

to know facts only in times of crisis.

[9] An interesting question is how does a sense-deprived person make aesthetic judgments pertaining to the organization they lead? For example, a top leader who is blind would lack the visual sense that sighted leaders rely on for analysis and decision-making. Likewise for a deaf leader, who would be unable to sense tone of voice or inflection. How does a sense-deprived leader comprehend the corporate culture, good or bad? How does a sense-deprived leader comprehend the built environment of luxury executive suites, office areas, or manufacturing shops? In what ways are aesthetic judgements included or excluded from analysis and decision-making? It seems reasonable to think that direct reports with full sense capabilities would stand in as proxies and supply aesthetic judgments to the leader where and when needed. This could be either good or bad. Alternatively, perhaps sense-deprived leaders could make better aesthetic judgments than fully sense capable direct reports because their perceptions are attuned differently. Sense-deprived leaders might be less beholden to traditions that sensory capable leaders view as indispensable, thus producing needed change.

[10] An organizations' culture is commonly viewed as resulting from leadership's behaviors. This book aims to show that aesthetics is the antecedent to leaders' behaviors and that aesthetics should be the point of focus (rather than leadership behaviors). It also explains, in a much simpler way, why people-centered culture is seen by most leaders as undesirable.

1

Hiding in Plain Sight

When we first experience something new or original, it quickly activates our senses and perceptual comprehension. That, in turn, and may stimulate wonderment, curiosity, and imagination, thus producing a memorable aesthetic experience, one that is positive or negative. In most cases, context and boundaries matter in relation to the experience. For example, seeing a highly acclaimed work of art in person, up close in a museum, evokes a sensory experience that is dramatically different than viewing the same work of art on a laptop computer screen. Similarly, those who begin their first day of work onsite at Apple Park in Cupertino, California, have a markedly different sensory experience entering the large circular "spaceship" building than those whose first day of work, and thereafter, is from a remote location.

If we encounter memorable aesthetic experiences again and again, they can become routine, even mundane, and their impact lessens. Routines hide aesthetic experiences. We go to work every day. We drive to work, cycle to work, walk to work, or work from home. We enter the workplace, go to our workstation, go to the bathroom, go to a meeting, go to lunch, do our tasks, and go home. How much do we really notice doing this day in and day out for years? Our senses become dulled for much of what we experience in the built environment, but we sense them nonetheless, perhaps taking a moment now and then to observe what is aesthetically pleasing or displeasing. Whether the experience is memorable or not, we are engaged in non-art, experienced-centered aesthetics rather than art-centered aesthetics.

We cannot dissociate ourselves from the built environment because it is part of the total sensory experience of social interaction in organizations. To do our work we interact with the building as well as functional objects such as computers, software applications, printers, machinery, desks, phones, as well as varied types of documents and workplace ephemera. These functional objects in themselves offer a multitude of sensory experiences. But for the purpose of aesthetic experience and aesthetic judgment, we must expand our understanding of objects to include other tangible objects such as people, what they wear, how they speak, tone of voice, facial expressions, and body movements, and intangible workplace objects such as data, information (tables, graphs, dashboards), knowledge, metrics, key performance indicators (KPIs), and user interfaces.

Other objects of aesthetic experience include activities such as doing one's assigned tasks, meetings, presentations, problem-solving, requests for information, helping others, etc. It also includes management systems, classical and progressive, which, along with the built environment, subsume all previously mentioned objects into an organized and coordinated whole. All these objects have associated with them qualities of both design and sensory experience. Day after day, these become the familiar, mundane objects of one's work and aesthetic experiences, but they are worth exploring further to understand their significance in forming aesthetic judgments.

Though mundane or at times seemingly inconsequential, these objects have meaning in people's work lives. Each tangible or intangible object, animate or inanimate, possesses different properties that can be thought of as variables in a large, complex, and undefinable equation. These properties are accounted for in human aesthetic experiences and in making aesthetic judgments. Combined, they provide the totality of sensory experience, causing heightened sensory experience in milliseconds, or dulling of sensory experience over time. The objects determine our satisfaction with varied aspects of work, which in turn influences our overall life experience, for better or worse.

Most often, our aesthetic experiences are deeply felt but not utilized individually or collectively as practical information to correct problems that cross economic, social, political, historical, philosophical, and spiritual (i.e., faith; beliefs or untested assumptions [1]) boundaries. In doing so, we give up a measure of control over our existence. We accept the aesthetic that someone else designed for us, one that likely perpetuates the status quo, and assume it is to our benefit. But, perhaps one day, we realize its deficiencies and consequences both personally and organizationally. Sooner or later, we realize what is lacking in the workplace with regard to respect, safety, helpfulness, compassion, and joy. We may realize the aesthetic that we have long accepted or approved of is not the humane environment that we had hoped it would be. And we likely do little to change it because we may feel disempowered.

This neglect of workplace aesthetics, the objects that inform our aesthetic experiences and our aesthetic judgments as beautiful or ugly, give power to the designers and actuators of workplace experience – those few people at the top of the hierarchy. This delimits motivation for action as well as the type and scope of action by every person in the organization. Consequently, our worldview is delimited by what others have designed for us to experience, and so we do not seriously consider alternative designs that offer improved sensory experiences that could result in improved outcomes for the organization and its stakeholders. Acceptance becomes compliance to aesthetic norms that could be outdated and thus no longer as useful as they once were. Imagination may still exist, but it is essentially idle because it cannot be acted upon to produce better aesthetic experiences that are current with the times we live in.

Generally, and in the context of classical management, it is advantageous for those at the top of the hierarchy to neglect workplace aesthetics, to keep it hidden or act like it is not there, for three reasons:

- If they are not concerned about workplace aesthetics, then most others below them will not be concerned
- The lack of concern for workplace aesthetics communicates to all that the existing aesthetic is acceptable or desirable
- Top leaders avoid having to think and take actions that could disrupt their existence personally and professionally, and thus avoid any risk of being wrong or socially ostracized

However, it is also generally true that the existing organizational aesthetic becomes less acceptable as one descends the hierarchy, but for reasons that may be difficult for people to articulate in specific ways. There may instead be abundant evidence of top-level problems such as low employee morale, poor teamwork, poor quality work, employee injuries, customer complaints, lawsuits, recalls, or other indicators of ugly dysfunction. And herein lies the problem with having a narrow view of aesthetics as pertaining only to visual arts or architecture. Any non-art object, including activities as objects that can be sensed and perceived, comprehended and experienced, becomes an aesthetic because it moves us in some way to an unequivocal judgment of beautiful or ugly. Understandably, that which serves the few, as opposed to the many, would be judged as beautiful by the few and ugly by the many [2].

Another way that an aesthetic serves the few is to conform to and perpetuate the viewpoint that leadership is an art, and thus, conversely, to deny any association of leadership with science (i.e., causality [3]). This bestows a potent privilege onto leaders to select whomever they like for promotion or to succeed them, as they are best to determine by sensory experience those most fit for advancement, inarguably so. Parallel to this aesthetic is another aesthetic, one in which people of similar mindset and capabilities to the leader are judged to be more worthy of advancement. The obvious consequence is a continuation of like-minded and often like-looking leaders imbued with inarticulable qualities that confirm their skills in the art of leadership. Given that sight, sound, and gut are the dominant senses used when making aesthetic judgments, this outcome is, of course, the most common one, and results in the continuing reduction of opportunities for women and minorities due to "lack of fit."

Recall the following portion of the definition of aesthetics presented in the Introduction:

> It considers what happens in our minds when we engage with aesthetic objects or environments such as viewing visual art, listening to music, reading poetry, **experiencing a play**, or exploring nature.

The words "experiencing a play" are worth further consideration. The daily activities of people in an organization can be seen as a performance given that most people's work performance is formally evaluated time to time by one's superiors. Some actors are highly attuned to organizational performance to keep their job or advance to higher levels. But others are less attuned or less concerned about performance, perhaps believing that they lack the control needed to secure their fate. Regardless, performative aspects of social interaction in the workplace, which includes sight and sound, must conform to a prescribed aesthetic to achieve desired ends. Some do this in an obsequious way, while others are more prudent or secretive.

The fact that organizations are political environments, and therefore concerned with appearances to greater or lesser extents, confirms its aesthetic foundation and edifice, and the ongoing importance of aesthetics and performance that supports the aesthetics. Because organizations and their leaders invariably have upward trajectories in terms of ambitions and measures, the aesthetics that supports these aims are revered while those that detract from it are scorned despite the reality that continuously upward trajectory is unrealistic and unnatural.

Figure 1-1 shows four graphs which could, for example describe, financial performance over a 12-month period. Only one graph (upper left) is judged to be beautiful by leaders because it smoothly and continuously increases. The remaining three charts are ugly: one is a flat line, the next is unpredictably up and down, and the last is declining. Seen this way, aesthetics helps to justify business decision-making.

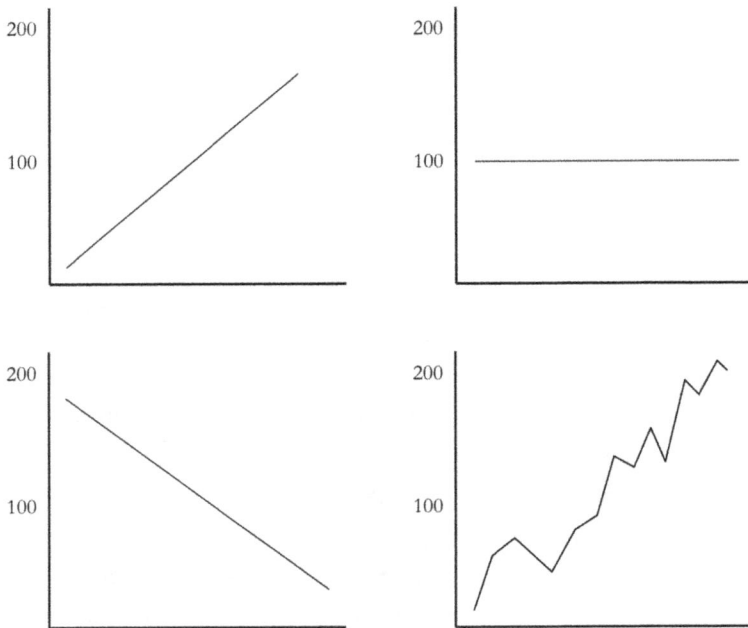

Figure 1-1. Aesthetics of charts. From upper left: beautiful chart, ugly chart (flat), ugly chart (declining), ugly chart (inconsistent).

It is easy to think of other examples such as the organization charts show in Figure 1-2. The aesthetically beautiful ones show the president at the top. Organization charts that are inverted, showing the president at the bottom, are aesthetically ugly – extremely ugly. The implication of an inverted organization chart is devastating. It suggests that the president is the lowest status person, and that the president works for the lowest-paid people at the top, when in fact most presidents view employees as working for them.

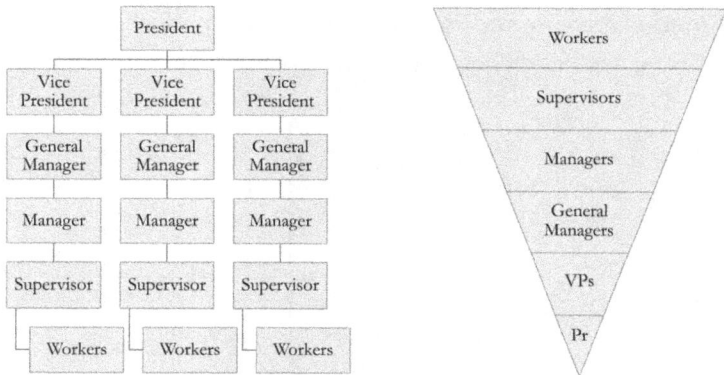

Figure 1-2. Aesthetically beautiful organization chart (left), and aesthetically ugly organization chart (right).

Given that certain aesthetics are cherished and cultivated while others are neglected over time, what are the long-term consequences of these choices for the organization, employees, and other stakeholders? It is difficult to say precisely because of the ways in which non-art objects inform aesthetic experiences and how aesthetic judgments vary over time, though some may be very stable because of expectations or traditions resulting from social learning across generations of leaders. Social norms and traditions at the top are highly influential and will generally subvert novel aesthetic experiences. What is the likelihood that the aesthetics that are cherished and cultivated by leaders are ones that do more harm than good, and those that are neglected could bring needed improvement to an organization and its employees? This is likely because times change and nothing lasts forever, not even aesthetic experiences judged by leaders for centuries to be beautiful.

We can think of an organization existing in its built environment, with its assemblage of leadership thinking and practices, management system, and other non-art aesthetic objects, as a self-contained unit unique to the social gathering of human beings pursuing a corporal mission, objectives, and goals. There is a seeming permanence to this experience-centered aesthetic because we tend to think that things last forever, or at least long enough to seem like forever. Leaders' perceptual field is personal and organizational survival. The boundaries that define the perceptual field are, at a high level, bracketed by threats and non-threats, with the threat of some type of loss being the principal focus. So, unimaginatively, aesthetic experiences must point in the direction of gain, that being judged beautiful, with attendant pretty charts to prove it.

Invariably, the leadership command is that gain must be continuously upward (beautiful), never downward (ugly), which places people in unrealistic situations and saddles then with unrealistic expectations, typically resulting in cognitive dissonance. Nonetheless, the pursuit of gain is assigned to various people at various levels of the organization. The expectation is that one will be totally successful in achieving the required gain because organizations, by their very nature, are success-oriented. Yet, many people fail to achieve their numbers – the required gain – and suffer in some way. It could be personal suffering from feeling guilty for having failed, despite perhaps not having been set up by management to succeed. They might be sidelined, demoted, or forced out of the organization. They might be fired. Recall this portion of the definition of aesthetics presented in the Introduction:

> …Aesthetics considers why people like some works of art and not others, as well as **how art can affect moods or even our beliefs**.

Non-art aesthetic experiences also affect moods and beliefs. In the case of not achieving one's numbers, the mood is not one of happiness. The person's guilt or displeasure with themselves for not having met organizational objectives weighs heavily on the mind. This depressing mood can enter the homelife and will be particularly troublesome to families if the source of cash for living is cut off. Such failure compels one to question their beliefs. Conversely, if one makes their numbers, the non-art aesthetic experiences affect moods and beliefs in opposite ways. The key point here is the aesthetic of gain (beauty) and loss (ugly) has profound impacts on people that are often deep and long-lasting, including among people in the organization who were not directly associated with producing the gain as well as outsiders.

The non-art aesthetic of gain drives people to be strongly attracted to those who somehow, time and time again, produce the required gain. They are seen as great leaders whose successes seem effortless and so great as to obscure all personal shortcoming or difficulties. This too is an aesthetic that is judged to be beautiful despite it being an unrealistic and incomplete comprehension of the facts. It is akin to our preference for certain types of images of landscapes such as majestic views of mountains or tropical beaches instead of mundane images of daily city, country, or home life. Our attention – the experience we prefer to have whether real or imagined – is drawn to the extraordinary, not the ordinary. And so we pay less attention to the ordinary. Yet it is the ordinary that so much of our aesthetic experience is derived and which we need to better understand. For if we look carefully at the ordinary, we begin to better understand how it influences our aesthetic experiences and judgments, and, consequently, our thinking and actions in organizations. In other words, the ordinary offers pathways for improving how organizations function.

Aesthetic judgments, even seemingly inconsequential ones, are significant in that they confer status to certain people, objects, and experiences. As such they can be used to proclaim the worth of people as well as a vast range of economic, social, political, historical, philosophical, business, and spiritual ideas and practices. The affirmation of beauty automatically and unambiguously defines ugliness. But more importantly, in defining beauty, it also defines its corollary, success, as well as its ugly opposite, failure. In doing so, a direction is clearly established for all to follow (Figure 1-3). Leaders "set direction," and the direction they set always points to beautiful. Leaders faithfully follow the "aesthetic compass," whether they know it or not, in the determined belief that it is absolute in its guidance and that beauty produces beautiful outcomes under all circumstances. This unbridled optimism is itself judged by leaders to be beautiful, which establishes the impossibility of it being invalid and thus ugly. As such, it cannot be falsified, thus giving great power and authority to leaders' aesthetic judgments – judgments that they want to see and want others to clearly see.

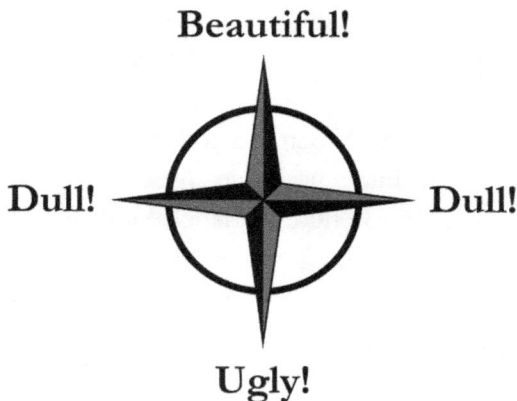

Figure 1-3. Classical management aesthetic compass. The exclamation points denote both the force of certitude that comes with status and the obligation to preserve the status quo.

This is why leaders can utter phrases such as "failure is not an option," "flawless execution," "grow or die," and the like with impunity. These esoteric, supernatural, phrases reflect an obsession with the unrealistic, status-based need to believe there are no problems (perfection) and pressures people to hide the truth, take shortcuts, or deceive [4]. The phrases compel the production of beautiful outcomes, whether they are in fact or not, and disrupt and negate individual and organizational learning because failure is not tolerated in success-oriented realms. Consequently, mistakes large and small are repeated within an organization, or the same or similar mistakes are repeated across organizations or industries [5]. Requiring outcomes to be beautiful cuts off the flow of information that warns of current mistakes and future problems, leading to another aesthetic that most leaders judge beautiful: blaming people lower in the hierarchy for problems.

The disruption and negation of individual and organizational learning that comes from leaders' attachment to and demand for beauty as the only outcome, coupled with that which is hiding in plain sight, is worth a much closer look. People are an organization's early warning system for problems. Remarkably, when corporate catastrophe happens, subsequent investigation reveals that many people, particularly those lower in the hierarchy, were long aware of the problems that led to the catastrophe and dutifully warned their bosses. And so, we perpetually wonder why warnings are not heeded. There is an explanation that lies within the realm of aesthetics.

When we think of top leaders, we often envision someone who is attractive, well dressed, articulate, experienced, and possesses worldly wisdom. We think of someone who drives an expensive car, wears expensive jewelry, owns a big house in an exclusive neighborhood, inhabits an elegant office, surrounds themselves with similarly beautiful people in similarly beautiful offices, and who enjoys the many beautiful benefits that come with high status. This description may be accurate or greatly exaggerated and is perhaps different for younger generations of leaders (casual attire, for example), but it rings true to the extent that someone atop the hierarchy is, in certain important ways, very different from people lower in the hierarchy. What about the people below? How do top leaders view those who toil away doing the actual work, day in and day out, producing what customers want? The hourly laborers and salaried personnel who work in the various functional areas of the company. Let's find out by visiting a manufacturing company.

It is rare for top leaders to visit the manufacturing shop floor for reasons other than hosting tours for politicians or important customers who are considering large purchases. Why is that? All one need do is see the manufacturing shop floor the way most top leaders might see it. Upon arrival they see a parking lot filled mostly with old cars. They enter a building, perhaps decades old and in need of paint and repairs. It is hot inside, and the air is thick with the stink of the various processes used to manufacture products. The factory ceilings are high and the space well-lit, but work areas seem messy and the floors dirty. They hear the noise of machinery, compressed air, forklifts, bells, sirens, and announcements paging this person or that. They see green, yellow, and red lights flashing, a jumble of exposed plumbing, piping, and electrical lines, and the stations where workers clock in and out to record their attendance and time to the minute. It is an unfamiliar and uncomfortable environment for most top leaders, perhaps because they spent their career in office jobs.

What else might the leaders see? They see people, the laborers, who make things, the goods and services that customers buy and the source of the company's cash. They see many old people, gray-haired or bald, and some young people, overweight people, and others with unkempt hair. People wearing worn-out shirts or tank tops that expose hairy arms, dense nests of armpit hair, and hairy shoulders. They see soiled pants and people who walk slowly due to back pain or a limp due to injury. Some wear short pants, exposing bowed legs and furry leg hair, and shoes that look ready to be thrown out. They see unshaven beards, dirty hands, and dirty fingernails, and people wearing safety equipment: earplugs, aprons, masks, gloves, goggles, respirators, and helmets. They see people bending over every minute or two, loading and unloading things, and sweating, and others standing for hours at a time assembling components. Some people smile, with teeth crooked or a tooth missing. They hear loud voices as people shout to be heard over the sound of the machinery and may overhear some people cursing.

The leaders visit the office area, plain and utilitarian. No fancy wall coverings, no carpeting, no mahogany desks, and no espresso machines. Cubicles with gray steel desks, made decades ago, resting on concrete, linoleum tile, or industrial carpet squares. People sit in worn, uncomfortable chairs, glued to their computer doing the same work every day. They hear the clatter of keyboards, ringing phones, conversations, and the noise of printers and copiers. No artwork adorns the walls, only safety posters and company notices. The office people dress casually, wearing inexpensive mass-produced clothes and shoes. They are in better physical shape and appearance overall than the factory laborers. They talk about their daily job and keeping the factory running, not profit and loss, free cash flow, return on net assets, or stock price. They are mundane middle-class salary people with simple lives and simple hobbies, slowly winding their way through a dull, if not ugly, work life that no executive wants for themselves or family members.

In visiting the factory, top leaders entered a strange, unfamiliar world, one so unlike their own that they cannot wait to leave. But it does not have to be a factory. It could be other, other disquieting environments such as an office, call center, bank branch, hotel property, farm, slaughterhouse, warehouse, chemical refinery, waste processing and recycling center, retail store, etc., housing the people who do the work. Far from being the majestic snow-capped mountain picture that is corporate headquarters, the shop and office is an aesthetically unattractive landscape; it is an ugly picture, more like an odorous swamp, hot desert, or barren prairie land where there is little to adore. What is important here is the aesthetic judgment that top leaders make about the people who do the work and the workplace itself. Leaders' experience of being on the shop floor and in the office areas, and seeing the people as aesthetically unappealing, affects their attitudes, analytical abilities, and decision-making.

The hourly labor and salaried staff who work there are needed means to a beautiful, profitable end, inclusive of executive cash salaries and bonuses, stock options, and perks – but no more. The inescapable impression made on most leaders is that these people, being ugly, have nothing to offer other than the exact job they were hired to do. They serve a mundane utilitarian purpose – do your job; nose to the grindstone; don't complain; be glad you have a job; if I want your input, I will ask for it – and they are seen as interchangeable and someday replaceable by technology. These people, both dull and too numerous, are dismissed based on an aesthetic judgment. Yet, these are the people whose abundance of innovative ideas, dedication, and pride keep the factory running and the business alive with customers' cash. And these are the people who know about problems that could multiply and easily topple the CEO and the stock price [6].

Leaders' aesthetic experience may not be perceived exactly as described here because some of it, perhaps much of it, is easy to gloss over. In fact, a leader may never visit a factory or office but instead have in mind a photograph, current or past, that produces an aesthetic judgment of that environment and its people as dull or ugly. Or, they may have heard about such workplaces from colleagues, parents, read about it in the newspaper, or simply harbor prejudice against workers. While some or many details may be missing, aesthetic judgments are made easily and quickly that those lower in the hierarchy are ugly – clearly in terms of personal appearance and workspace, but more importantly in terms of their capacity to think, understand what is going on, solve problems, and offer informed warnings of impending peril. This being the case, it is apparent that workers cannot be trusted – they are a threat to beauty – and so they must be closely surveilled to assure they produce the required results.

When these ugly people inform leaders the facts about problems that need to be corrected, recognizing that only top leaders can correct certain problems, they are usually ignored [7]. In this way, aesthetic judgments block the flow of accurate information and hide problems for months, years, or decades. Instead, the aesthetic compass points to one direction, beauty, which means those at the top, and merely because they are at the top, possess right thinking, right understanding, and right decision-making capabilities, and thus believe they have no need to know about problems emanating from below [8] – that is until catastrophe strikes. When that happens, the aesthetic judgments previously made about lower-level people consigns them to be blamed for problems that top leaders did not want to know about or refused to acknowledge. This and related aesthetic judgments forcefully signal status; mine is greater than yours, and as such the leaders enjoy certain rights and privileges that workers will never experience.

Blaming people for problems is a manifestation of the larger realm of neglect that most leaders have for the everyday workings (aesthetics) of the organization below the senior level of the organization (CEO, president, vice president, and general manager). They know not and care not for the ugly details of the work – the processes people work in and manage – whether carried out in honest and exacting ways or corrupted by shortcuts to quickly produce the appearance of beautiful results that the boss demands to see. If person A does not produce the desired result, then person B takes over, followed by person C, and so on, until the beautiful result is achieved or no longer needed. When people below demand changes in leadership and management thinking or practice, or if such demands are made from outsiders (investors, regulators, suppliers), those demands will likely go unheard because the source is ugly, obtrusive, and annoying. To a great extent, they are barred from providing input to management decision-making. If changes are made, they will be made on leaders' terms and will be small and mostly symbolic to maintain the required leadership aesthetic of shrewd authority and tight control to deny infringement on their rights and privileges.

The foregoing has described how aesthetic experiences and aesthetic judgments, whether hiding in plain sight or not, can inform leadership thinking and decision-making to a much greater extent than we realize, and whether and what types of progress are made. In particular, how aesthetic experiences and aesthetic judgments – the raw motivations for leadership action and inaction – advance or retard progress in top leaders' thinking and practice of leading and managing organizations. The next chapter examines the aesthetics of classical management to explain why it endures [9] despite the existence of progressive alternatives that are better suited for current times and needs.

"They are wise who can see what is good about what they dislike and can see what is bad about what they like."

- Zen proverb

Ideas for Improvement

List some ideas to improve aesthetic experiences for employees and other stakeholders. Try out your ideas.

•

•

•

•

•

•

Notes

[1] The meaning of "spiritual" as used in this book is non-religious. Its means things that people working in organizations believe in without testing if the belief is true or not. It is to accept assumptions without validation. It can include implicit rules, customs, routines, and traditions. Beliefs and assumptions can fall within the realm of superstition, the mystical or occult. Examples include: the "invisible hand" of the market, simplistic solutions to complex problems, avoidance of facts, success-orientation (and evasion of failure), faith in metrics and KPIs as trustworthy information for decision-making, forecasts, etc. To further understand the role of spirituality in leadership and management, see Emiliani, B. (2020), *Management Mysterium: The Quest for Progress*, Cubic LLC, South Kingstown, Rhode Island

[2] Some lower in status may view that which serves the few at the top of the hierarchy as beautiful because their aspire to those realms. Others may view that which serves the few at the top of the hierarchy as dull due to disinterest, the unlikelihood of making it to the top, or that matters which concern those at the top are tedious or debilitating.

[3] Emiliani, B. (2015), *Speed Leadership: A New Way to Lead for Rapidly Changing Times*, The CLBM, LLC Wethersfield, Connecticut

[4] Corporate strategy is usually a construction of imagined and unrealistic targets designed by leaders to achieve

outcomes they judge to be beautiful. Typically, the people lower down the organization who are charged with achieving the targets encounter difficulties such that the top leaders' vision of beauty is not realized. To preserve one status, honor, and authority, leaders blame people, external parties, or external events for failure.

[5] Emiliani, B. and Torinesi, M. (2021), *Wheel of Fortune: Getting to the Heart of Business Strategy*, Cubic LLC, South Kingstown, Rhode Island

[6] It is noteworthy that leaders age well compared to workers in the sense that leaders with decades of experience are more highly valued than workers with decades of experience. The former is aesthetically perceived as having gained an attractive patina while the latter has gained an ugly, damaging rust that warrants disposal. The categorization and valuing of present to past exposes a lack of insight and appreciation, as well as managerial negligence. The challenge is learning how to gain a positive aesthetic appreciation for what appears to be aged, withered, less capable, and thus no longer useful. To not do so it to maintain the status quo and the socio-economic preconceptions that single out certain people for differential treatment that they never asked for.

[7] In classical management, logic and logical arguments, and facts, are generally seen by leaders to be ugly and cumbersome aesthetics, and thus often ignored. It is the leader's prerogative to ignore the reality of any situation that they find annoying or troublesome, in large part to maintain and expand the aesthetic of personal and organizational

status and success. The determined efforts to produce and maintain the success aesthetic functions as a moral justification for one's status and dominance, as well as the organization's continued existence. The success aesthetic also aids in justifying the continuing need for in-groups and out-groups, which has the dual outcome of perpetuating the status quo and limiting opportunities for others.

[8] In most leaders' view, the problems that occur on the shop or office floor are unimportant, trivial, and ugly, and thus not worthy of their attention. The problems that leaders face pertain mostly to strategy and finance and are seen by them as large, important, and beautiful. The inability or antipathy to see the close connection between the ugly problems on the shop and office floor and the beautiful problems of strategy and finance results from leaders' privilege to waive responsibility for problems.

[9] It seems a contributing factor to the endurance of classical management over the last 40 years is market concentration and associated financialism, shareholder focus, and executive compensation (thank you to Jeff Morrow for raising this point). As organizations grow larger, become fewer in number, and gain greater market share, there is rapidly diminishing incentive for top leaders to shift to a new system of management. Innovations in management thinking and methods are muted or extinguished, preferring instead for any changes to be closely aligned with the current classical management method. However, among leaders schooled in classical management, progressive management is generally seen as undesirable under any circumstance.

2

Aesthetics of Classical Management

Where does our understanding of management come from? Most people would think it comes from the workplace or from college courses. But in fact, our understanding of management is informed by many earlier experiences. These include family [1], membership in the church, K-12 education, participation in youth sports, club memberships, boy or girl scouts, and the like [2]. These experiences are our first exposure to management. An older person – parent or coach, priest or teacher – organizes the activities of young children. Whether they realize it or not, young children learn the fundamentals of management; the thinking and ways of doing things that are rooted in traditions that the adult learned when they were young, going back untold generations. These basic forms of management become the foundation on which professional management is built, where "professional" means the people who are compensated for the purpose of managing an organization's people and processes and have work titles such as supervisor, manager, general manager, vice president, president, or CEO.

Socially inherited understandings of management imbue young people with scores of preconceptions about management. This, coupled with inductive reasoning, produces generalizations about management, ones that are not necessarily based on having personal experience managing other people. As people grow older and enter the workforce, they join the ranks of the professionally managed. They learn what it is like to be professionally managed and to exist within a hierarchy of professional managers. Over time, these experiences may be generally consistent with what they experienced as youth, in their family, in school, or in extracurricular activities. As employees compensated for their work, they may or may not like the experience of existing within a hierarchy of professional managers, but most come to accept it as the standard that they must accept and adjust to out of necessity.

Some will be promoted to supervisor while others will ascend further up the hierarchy. Along the way, they will face the challenge of conforming to the preconceptions and methods of management required by senior managers that is common to most organizations, classical management. Over the course of many years, they will become highly skilled at the practice of classical management through a combination of social learning and personal practice. Having fully absorbed the shared thinking and practice of classical management, they will see newer methods of management – if they see them at all – as unusual. Will leaders be curious to learn more about a management system that deviates from the norm? Or will the aesthetics of classical management that they have long experienced and long ago judged to be both good and right, and thus beautiful, prevail over any consideration to learn progressive management thinking and practice?

The likely outcome is that leaders will remain committed to classical management. But what is the specific mechanism by which that decision is made? With these six starting points,

- Aesthetics socially inherited in one's youth
- Preconceptions about people, management, etc.
- Cognitive biases and stereotypes
- Personal experience with classical management
- Social learning absorbed from superiors
- Knowledge of the facts and fictions of the ends of business,

one's mind has been prepared to engage in inductive reasoning; to develop general principles that have a probability of being correct. This would clearly be in preference to deductive reasoning because deductive reasoning requires effort to be expended (i.e., experiments and trial and error) to determine the validity of hypotheses. Most managers, especially senior-level managers, are not likely to do that because of their status and thus the nonessential need for certainty that follows from correct premise to conclusion in deductive reasoning [3]. Therefore, judgments of progressive management will nearly always proceed on the basis of inductive reasoning. For most leaders, a high probability of being correct, based on the six points listed above, is good enough for most decision-making. It produces correct, beautiful decisions without having to expend much thought. Additionally, top leaders have been rigorously selected over time for their capacity to make "right" decisions.

So how does it work? Inductive reasoning relies on patterns to establish the premise on which conclusions, are based. Figure 2-1 shows a simple pattern of numbers. Inductive reasoning quickly suggests that the missing number in the

6 6 6 6 6 6 6 6 6 6 __ 6 6

Figure 2-1. Simple pattern of numbers.

pattern should be six – a very high probability that the number is six. Most people would be confident about that thematically consistent conclusion and see no need to engage in time-consuming deductive experiments via the scientific method to test the validity of guesses. But there is a non-zero probability that the missing number is not six, but two. That would surprise most people. Surprises often happen in executive decision-making because the patterns they rely on to make decisions may not be the patterns that occur in reality due to the exclusion of information. While executive experience is judged to be useful as sets of patterns for confidently predicting the future, it has limitations.

If we substitute the numbers in Figure 2-1 with the letters "CM" for classical management, we create a pattern in which classical management seems to be constantly occurring. It seems there is a high probability that CM should fill the void in the pattern. But what if the void is filled with "PM," progressive management? That would disconfirm the pattern. But would a seemingly random break in the pattern introduce uncertainty in the mind of leaders as to the worth of long-lived classical management? Most likely it would not because an aesthetic judgment based on aesthetic experiences have been rendered long ago.

CM   CM   CM   CM   CM   __   CM   CM

Figure 2-2. Inductive generalization.

One who is hopeful might expect the following to occur:

CM Leader → New PM Information
→ CM Pattern Disconfirmed → Make Changes

A leader experienced in classical management comes across information about progressive management, sees an opportunity for "change for the better," and then proceeds to make significant changes to the organization's leadership and management practice. But this rarely happens. Instead, something different occurs:

CM Leader → New PM Information
→ CM Pattern Disconfirmed → ~~Make Changes~~
→ Generate Theory of Inadequacy of PM

A leader experienced in classical management comes across information about progressive management, sees an opportunity for "change for the better," does not make any changes due to a preference for the status quo, and then proceeds to develop a theory of inadequacy of progressive management that will include these imputations:

- Takes too long
- Does not work
- We're different
- Costs too much money
- We're too busy
- Our work varies too much
- It is too complicated

The leader's untested theory of inadequacy of progressive management, derived inductively based on a conflicting aesthetic judgment, overrides all factual evidence of the superiority of progressive management. Nevertheless, there is a probability that the leader is correct; that progressive management is inferior (ugly) compared to beautiful classical management. There will be no deductive testing – no experimenting with progressive management – to avoid the great risk of proving the leader wrong (ugly), a loss of status (uglier), and to strengthen in the minds of everyone the utility and worth of classical management. The theory of inadequacy is put forward with 100 percent certainty, despite its inductive origins rooted in classical management, resulting in the status quo. From leaders' perspective, whatever is, is right, and thus beautiful.

Consequently, whatever technological or social idea, tool or method that aligns with classical management is easily accepted by leaders with few or no questions. In this way, classical management reveals its path dependence. Decisions leaders make are consistent with past experiences and decisions, thus sustaining the aesthetic of classical management. Conversely, progressive management is a significant break from path dependence. It is an ugly aesthetic because it represents both technological changes and social changes that are inconsistent with classical management. The system, structure, order, and hierarchy of classical management, accepted and understood for centuries, eliminates many mysteries and questions. In doing so, it induces feelings of satisfaction and peace of mind. Progressive management upsets that understanding and peace of mind and produces a displeasing disruption, an unwanted challenge to leaders' previously ratified aesthetic judgments of beauty.

The aesthetics of classical management define an acceptable range of beauty. Progressive management lies outside these aesthetic boundaries. The practical effect is to reject curiosity about progressive management's mindset and methods to prevent disharmony and maintains the status quo. Yet what most leaders don't realize is the extent to which classical management retards progress. Circa 1910, the great industrial engineer Henry Gantt said [4]:

"The usual way of doing a thing is always the wrong way."

These words, taken to heart, would have leaders at any level of an organization question their preconceptions, methods, and decisions in a productive way that would lead to needed changes that are in step with the times. Yet few leaders subscribe to Henry Gantt's words because it is the wrong aesthetic. It is an ugly aesthetic full of sadness and frustration because it asks leaders to confront the fact that classical management may contain many problems that they have long ignored or do not recognize. The patterns that they have come to know and accept through inductive reasoning reveal a substantial probability of having been wrong. This cuts to the heart of one's being as a leader – status, honor, power, influence, rights, and privileges – and is obviously very disturbing.

The course of action taken by most leaders is to conform to

orthodoxy and redouble their commitment to classical management, thus retaining their pragmatic, worldly wisdom outlook. In doing so, they maintain the right to lead and manage as they please, guided by gut intuition and rule of thumb, and do as nearly all other leaders do. There is no allure to adopting Henry Gantt's skepticism and lead by facts rather than by right, to unlearn classical management and learn progressive management, to improve one's observation skills or imagination, or to undertake a dynamic, evolutionary perspective of leadership and management. From Gantt's perspective, whatever is, is wrong, and thus ugly.

There is a marked contrast between leadership by right, classical management, and leadership by facts, progressive management [5]. They are vastly different aesthetics that result in different understandings and orderings of social and technical phenomena. Progressive management is rooted in the scientific and engineering perspective of experimentation and trial and error, while classical management reflects a business or deal-making (trading) perspective rooted in social relations to achieve some form of gain. Proficiency in these result from different types of training and learning. Figure 2-3 depicts the social learning process, which is much easier to learn compared to the scientific method [6].

It begins with tenacious beliefs that are formed early in one's youth in the management of the family, school, or extracurricular activity. As one gets older and starts to work for a living, we enter a hierarchy where an authority, the top leader, sets direction. We appeal to authority and tradition to confirm our tenacious beliefs and become confident of the natural order – i.e., whatever is, is right. The

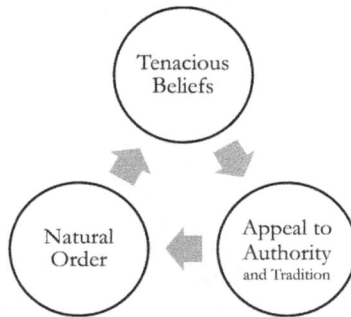

Figure 2-3. Social learning process.

social learning process is very effective in part because it makes use of "carrots and sticks" which engages the limbic part of the brain (emotional or feeling part) and the brain stem (reptilian or instinct) that precede thought. If one does not conform, then one faces a painful loss of social standing. In this way, leaders maintain the social status quo to achieve their desired ends. But more importantly, this perpetuates scores of economic, social, political, historical, philosophical, business, and spiritual preconceptions, thus entrenching classical management.

Figure 2-4 depicts the learning via the scientific method, which is much more challenging and protracted pathway for learning compared to social learning, one that requires years of rigorous education and practice. Rather than acting on the limbic system and brain stem, engagement with the scientific method engages the neocortex, the higher-order brain functions for sensory perception, cognition, and reasoning. The focus is cognition of problems, curiosity to understand

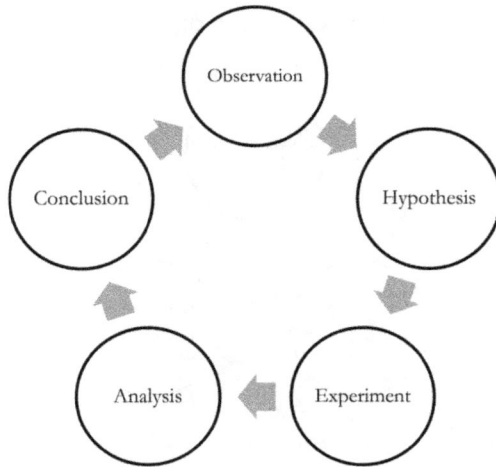

Figure 2-4. Learning via the scientific method.

cause-and-effect, and problem-solving, which results in learning and improvement, and destroys preconceptions. Rather than being strictly focused on ends, scientific thinkers are concerned about means as well as ends. However, they are not isolated from social learning; it is part of their lived experience. Yet, the illogic and cognitive biases that are pervasive in social learning in hierarchical organizations typically causes much personal confusion and turmoil. That is because there is intrinsic antagonism between pragmatism and scientific thinking [7], and so the former has a higher probability of prevailing in organizations than the latter.

Classical management's aesthetics is a simplistic way of thinking that fulfills a pragmatic vision. It works in the "real world" as one can plainly see, though it oversimplifies complex problems and has within it a structural bias against reform (reform being ugly). Consequently, Henry Gantt's maxim, "The usual way of doing a thing is always the wrong way," is plainly unacceptable. The ugly disorder, chaos, complexity, and strangeness that appeals to progressive management's scientific logical thinkers as alluring problems to solve is wholly unappealing to the devotees of classical management who crave the beauty of order, harmony, simplicity, and familiarity (recall Pollock's and Vermeer's works cited in the Introduction). A disturbing change in aesthetics is nearly impossible to "sell" to leaders because it is a matter of beauty and taste, which is instrumental, and thus cannot be justified by a clearly identifiable truth.

Only rarely is the chasm bridged because leaders' aesthetic judgments tend to be permanent. It is not a case like taking a music appreciation course wherein someone who previously disliked hip-hop/rap music undergoes a change of heart and mind. More typically, leaders think and make decisions which signal that order and prosperity requires more of doing the same in the future as what has been done in the past. And so, traditions prevail. The specific values that inform the aesthetic of status quo oriented classical management include:

- Tradition
- Coherence
- Conformity
- Completeness
- Certainty
- Consistency
- Comfort
- Structure

- Safety
- Stability
- Meaning
- Purpose
- Authority

While leaders may view classical management as imperfect, and perhaps may even dislike it, the alternative, progressive management, is seen as much worse. Leaders generally see it as upending most or all that they know and producing unwanted social problems in their peer group. They distrust the new, so they impute myriad faults. But this is not the fault of anyone, and so there is no one to blame. Nature imbues humans with socially constructed aesthetic sensibilities and weakness for the types of preconceptions and predictions (inductive reasoning) that bring order to complex life situations. Socially accepted beauty in relation to the ends of business perpetuates classical management. Aesthetics, then, is a simpler theory to explain the static way in which most organizations have been led and managed by generations of leaders. In particular, a theory that explains why most leaders resist, reject, or ignore progressive management. From this, we can establish a Law of Common Leadership:

When confronted with a problem, the principal solution set will be based on an aesthetic judgment of beauty.

This contrasts with progressive management where the principal solution set is based on facts [8], with the result being the correction of problems at the source. These improvements allow an organization to keep up with changing times.

What are some of the consequences of perpetuating classical management in times better suited for progressive management [9]?

- Non-management employees – shop and office workers – whose work is rooted in the world of facts, are required to conform to the leader's aesthetics. This makes it more difficult for them to do their work and leads to confusion, frustration, and employee turnover. In short, classical management is bad for employees [10] but is very good for leaders.

- The classical management aesthetic assures that organizations remain behind the times. They are perpetually reactive, rather than proactive in response to changing social and technical [11] conditions. This result in a reduction in competitive capabilities over time and greater expenditure (or waste) of the various resources that leaders claim to be scarce [12].

- The organization fails, to greater or lesser extents, to fulfill its mission and serve the needs of society to the extent that it could. This can leave employees feeling less fulfilled and may motivate them to find jobs elsewhere.

- The organization becomes more vulnerable to outside forces: sales declines, loss of employee engagement and knowledge, employee turnover, leadership turnover, becoming a takeover target, or going bankrupt.

Owing to these consequences, it is wise for leaders to periodically examine their aesthetic experiences and aesthetic judgments. They should test their inductive generalizations [13] and pay attention to changes in patterns that suggest the need for revising or abandoning one's aesthetics. This must come from within because of the difficulty outsiders have in getting leaders to like aesthetics they deeply dislike or distrust [14]. To succeed, leaders must overcome their own special interests and be willing to contend with the consequences.

Classical management represents a standard of leadership and management practice that fulfilled the specific needs of a time and place. It has existed for so long that it has become customary and proprietary to the interests of leaders such that any attempts at significant change are blocked. Classical management is maladaptive to change, and its devotees have lost sight of its original intent and purpose. Consequently, most leaders will fervently defend obsolete ways of thinking and doing things because of their long-lived aesthetic experiences and a hardening of their aesthetic judgments. They are shields planted firmly against progress.

Leaders are secure in the rigidity of status quo and troubled by a changing world that requires them to be flexible and adaptive [15]. These sentiments can be exploited to gain broad support for archaic organizational values and obsolete aesthetic judgments, failing in themselves, and others, to dispense with illusions. Often, this presents itself as leaders' sociopathic use of aesthetics to achieve personal and business gain, particularly money and status, under the guise of rectitude. The antidote to this counterproductive habit of mind is to engage the material world through human sensory perceptions firmly and thoughtfully attuned to facts, and to recognize that acceptance of ugly disorder, chaos, complexity, and strangeness – the facts of reality, rather than appearance of beauty – lead to quicker adaptation to both small changes and crises as well as the development of emergent capabilities that better serve the organization and its stakeholders.

· · · · · · · ·

"Virtually all thoughtful persons… will agree that it is a despicably inhuman thing for the current generation willfully to make the way of life harder for the next generation…"

- Thorstein Veblen

Ideas for Improvement

List some ideas to improve aesthetic experiences for
employees and other stakeholders. Try out your ideas.

-

-

-

-

-

-

Notes

[1] Le Texier, T. (2013), "The First Systematized Uses of the Term 'Management' in the Eighteenth and Nineteenth Centuries," *Journal of Management History*, Vol. 19, No. 2, pp. 189-224

[2] Within this realm, certain youth may be called upon by the adult "manager" to represent his or her peers, for example as a captain of a youth sports team. In such roles, the youth would have a closer connection to and interaction with the adult manager. Additionally, the young captain would perform an auxiliary management and leadership role to team members, thus gaining "management" experience in a non-professional setting. Such experience may prove useful later in life if one becomes a professional manager. It could also prove to be a great liability later in life if one becomes a professional manager owing to the scores of preconceptions about leading and managing people that one has gained from adult manager(s). For example, a youth sports team captain may assign lesser roles to peers that to not meet certain aesthetic criteria. The aesthetic, formed early in life, could easily be carried on into one's professional life, thus denying capable people of opportunities for growth or advancement.

[3] Add to that top leaders' proclivity to blame lower-level people for their mistakes, which further enhances the appeal of inductive reasoning over deductive reasoning. The latter type of reasoning is the domain of people lower in the hierarchy; shop and office workers.

[4] Copley, F.B. (1923), *Frederick W. Taylor: Father of Scientific Management*, Volume 1, The Taylor Society, New York, New York, p. 112

[5] Emiliani, B. (2018), *The Triumph of Classical Management Over Lean Management: How Tradition Prevails and What to Do About It*, Cubic LLC, South Kingstown, Rhode Island

[6] Classical management is so easy to learn that most people who have been rigorously trained in science, engineering, or liberal arts critical thinking quickly abandon that learning and replace it with the social learning process that generates and sustains classical management. This social contagion effect quickly aligns mindsets and behaviors away from facts and favors closed-mindedness, loyalty over expertise, and perpetuation of the regime. The aesthetic appeal of classical management is what makes it so popular, as do its simplistic causal relationships such as supply and demand and blaming people for problems, as well as simplistic prescriptions such as economies of scale to achieve lower costs, technology as the solution to improve efficiency and eliminate labor problems, and the privilege of not having to learn from previous errors. Control is more highly valued than whatever the organization produces. This acquiescence to tradition, authority, and falsehoods functions as a type of religion that rightly confounds those who work or hope for progress.

[7] In any political realm such as business or government, pragmatic thinking, rigidly in alignment with expediency and self-interest, generally prevails over scientific thinking because of the need to maintain status and pretense for the

purpose of survival. Scientific thinking (facts, cause-and-effect) has zero respect for status, pretense, traditions, vested rights and privileges, etc. That is why scientific thinking is so dangerous to leaders' power, authority, and influence. Yet leaders, being shrewd, know that given a choice, most people will forgo facts for rhetoric (often combined with misinformation) as shown in the image below. The social and emotional power of Choice #1, wherein beliefs may be misrepresented as facts, usually exceeds the social and emotional power of Choice #2 – often to the detriment of people lives and livelihoods.

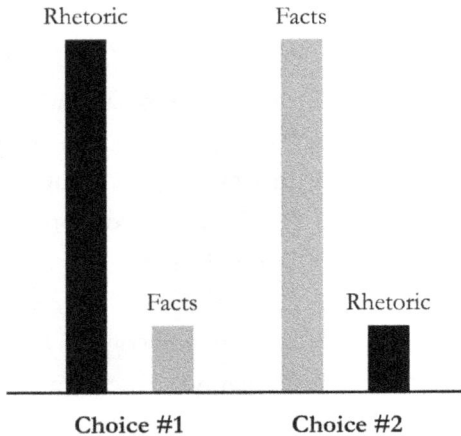

[8] It is noteworthy that when disaster strikes, top leaders of an organization can no longer avoid the facts. They must abandon the metaphysical realm of classical management and the Institution of Leadership (see Note 5) and deal with the problem in the material realm. See Emiliani, B. and Torinesi, M. (2021), *Wheel of Fortune: Getting to the Heart of Business Strategy*, Cubic LLC, South Kingstown, Rhode Island

[9] Classical management, with roots dating to the late Middle Ages and before, is unfit for the 21st century. The needs of humanity are increasingly of the type that classical management, narrow in its focus and benefits, cannot provide. Consequently, there is a need to transition from a privilege-based management system to a reality- and human-based management system that develops diverse people to be more adept at recognizing and solving problems quickly. The rapidly changing digital era that we now live in, coupled with changing social needs and existential environmental and geopolitical threats, demands such a change. If these aesthetics are ignored, then classical management will continue to prevail.

[10] As evidenced by "The Great Resignation," job switching caused by job dissatisfaction (low pay, poor or no benefits, poor working conditions, disrespect, poor supervision, poor leadership, etc.). See https://en.wikipedia.org/wiki/Great_Resignation, accessed 2 March 2022

[11] An organization could be technologically in arrears due to no investment, insufficient investment, over-investment, incorrect investment, or some combination of these.

[12] Most leaders are highly skilled at creating or perpetuating imaginary or an imagined aesthetic that the organization is always teetering on the edge of existence. An obvious example is when managers declare there is no money for what regular employees need, but there is ample money for increases in executive pay and benefits or purchasing expensive new automation technologies. Such rhetoric

succeeds as an aesthetic. Unsurprisingly, many policies and rules are created to preserve a traditional aesthetic of management control over workers.

[13] This chapter does not advise against inductive reasoning. Rather, it points out that people in leadership positions use inductive reasoning in ways that can lead to incorrect general conclusions, rigidly adhered owing to the need to maintain status, which can affect other people in negative ways.

[14] Leaders like to make up their own minds and strongly dislike being challenged about things or being channeled into things that are at variance with their views. This may be true of most people, but it is particularly troublesome to people in leadership positions, from supervisor to CEO. People in these positions have a great need for certainty and for being right, despite the impossibility of these being fulfilled. That is because being wrong is seen to be the same as failing or losing. This closes off avenues for making progress.

[15] When a perception settles in that leadership and management are too complex, perhaps by a changing world or other factors, leaders revert to what is both more familiar (based on the past) and simpler to understand and do. Similarly, when workers seek progressive reform, leaders' inclinations move in the opposite direction. Both of these situations favor the continuation of classical management. Action-reaction; the human physics of social hierarchies.

3

Management Design

One can readily imagine that many different forms and systems of management have existed at different times during the last several thousand years. Most were short-lived while some were long-lived. Over the past few hundred years, it seems that most innovations in management soon faded away and were replaced with traditional management thinking and practice [1]. The common threads in all organizations are hierarchy and atomized aesthetic judgments, and so these, along with a human propensity for domination [2], seem to be among the primary driving forces for reversion to management's most basic design, classical management – an aesthetic that is patriarchal in its origin.

Classical management is of a particular design that is rooted in the past for the purpose of fulfilling the specific needs of people, time, and place. It was not designed *a priori* on a piece of paper and then implemented. Instead, it emerged from the needs of leaders, their early influences, habits of mind, and to sustain social institutions that benefit leaders. Classical management emerged from the realm of self-interest and the viewpoint that what was good for the leader would be good (or good enough) for all others. The narrowness of self-interest necessarily excludes serious consideration of persons far removed from the leader's inner circle. Those people exist to support the leader's reign, not for the leader to support the larger populations' existence so that they may fully flower as human beings.

This raises the question, are the precepts that delineate classical management and its associated aesthetic experiences and aesthetic judgments still valid in the 21st century? And for whom: leaders or workers? It seems clear that the precepts which delineate classical management have had diminished appeal for workers over the last 40-plus years and for some leaders, but not for most leaders. Consequently, there has been determined efforts by leaders to thwart the dismantling of classical management, and such efforts will likely continue in the future because it maximizes leaders' rights and privileges. As economic historian Douglas Dowd said [3]:

"'What's next' is most likely to be determined by what *is*."

Should we succumb to this fatalist view, or should we consider constructing an aesthetic experience that defines beauty in a way that leaders might not like as much as classical management, but which increasing numbers of leaders might be able to live with – or forced to live with due to changes in workplace and societal values or environmental or geopolitical conditions requiring more highly engaged workforces? Consider a management system as an organized and consistent set of principles and practices, and the system as an object that is comprised of various design features that make it easy or difficult for humans to experience. Who designs management systems? They are designed collectively over time by people, principally those in leadership positions, with adjustments made periodically that are generally aligned with previously established principles and practices. The human tendency to build on what has previously been accepted assures that progress lags far behind the   actual needs of individuals and society.

The designers of an object, be it a cell phone, kitchen appliance, automobile, building, or management system hold great power in terms of the how the object is experienced by its users or those who are affected by the user's experience. Designers have a great impact, more than most realize, in shaping aesthetic experiences. They must think beyond the object produced to the effects that it has on people and on things, both favorable and unfavorable. Classical management hardly incorporates such considerations. Oftentimes it can be as bad for leaders as it is for workers and other stakeholders, albeit in different ways [4]. Thinking of a management system as an object helps make something that is abstract more specific and tangible. Seeing it represented as an object forms an image in the mind that aids in its comprehension. The image below is a tetrahedron which we will use to represent classical management.

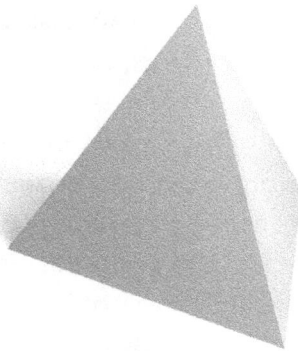

Figure 3-1. Object representing classical management.

The prominent features of this design are sharp edges, sharp angles, sharp peak, and stable triangular base. Sharp features are generally considered ugly. Its geometrical minimalism evokes the Brutalist style of architectural design. The sharpness of the object representing classical management is suggestive of "sharp practice," which was a term used a century ago to describe harmful zero-sum ways of interacting with stakeholders. "Sharp practice" as a daily occurrence in the management of people and processes was frowned upon by progressive managers because it made getting the job done more difficult in every way. It undercut teamwork in the organization and cooperation with and between external stakeholders such as customers and suppliers, which results in delays, higher costs, quality problems, etc. Anyone with experience in organizations today know the truth of this. The purpose of management is to organize people and other resources to produce a product or service (an experience) that satisfies a want or need. Given the fundamentally human orientation of management, it would seem out of place for management to produce experiences and outcomes that are harmful to people – the primary stakeholders: employees, customers, suppliers, investors, and communities.

"Sharp practice" is out of place in benign (non-warfare) human activity in organizations, yet the very design of the classical management system assures that "sharp practice" is the standard and that errors and mistakes will occur every day, by every leader, at all levels of leadership [5]. Of course, external factors are always present, but to a remarkable extent the management system itself facilitates generating a flood of errors and mistakes [6] due to leaders lacking awareness of their inconsistencies, not testing beliefs and assumptions, pervasive use of illogical thinking, and the existence of cognitive biases – plus, a general unwillingness to learn the root cause of errors as this would diminish one's status and authority [4]. Simply put, it is a bad design.

The sharp peak at the top of the classical management tetrahedron clearly suggests the existence of a hierarchy. It is true that organizations need leaders, but many top leaders love the title, compensation, and privileges far more than they like the fetid work of leading people. This is apparent by leaders' physical distance from workers, lack of engagement with workers, their disinterest in workers' problems, and the often strictly performative aspects of employee engagement. Hierarchies are thought to be enabling of good work, yet in most cases it disables that which produces consistently good work: questioning beliefs and assumptions, challenging illogical thinking and cognitive biases, and learning the root cause of errors and mistakes – whether at the bottom or top of the organization. Not wanting one's status and authority challenged is not without costs, costs that will surely become obvious in the long run.

Actually doing the human-oriented work of leadership and management is much less appealing than enjoying the rights, privileges, power, and special relationships that come with being a top leader. Yet, persistently ignoring employees, their work, and their processes, and assuming others are properly tending to them, is to invite problems that will surely frustrate top leaders. They cannot understand why things do not go as planned in the execution of strategy and tactics. They become angry and wrathful due to cost, quality, and delivery problems, blame lower-level managers and workers, or whole departments, for these problems. They look to replace or eliminate people or close non-performing sites. They look to outsource work to suppliers who they believe will do a better job, for no other reason than the suppliers said so in their response to the request for proposal. And they ignore employee survey data that finds persistently low morale, employee turnover, and related human resource problems because such facts are annoying, inconvenient, and not easily corrected within the realm of classical management.

The political environment in organizations with these kinds of problems is sharp. There is infighting among members of the executive team and managers below. It invites psychopathic behaviors and produces fear and psychological harm to people throughout the hierarchy. While perhaps a form of workplace entertainment for some, the consequence is to lose sight of customer wants and needs, likely resulting in financial and other problems. Organizational politics diverts leaders' attention from fulfilling the company's purpose to satisfy customers. It prevents leaders from seeing the reality of both internal and external environments. It stunts human growth, development, and learning, and wastes time and other resources. It serves no purpose other than to selfishly elevate one's status at the expense of others.

The base of the classical management tetrahedron is wide and stable, and thus difficult to move. The great force needed to move it assures continuity with long-established ("settled") aesthetic judgments such that significant change is very difficult. The management system design does not allow it.

Leaders adjust the design through various initiatives, but path dependence assures that the result is largely the same – status quo. Because there are few alternatives, most employees have little choice but to endure this ugly aesthetic experience. Classical management is needlessly sharp, needlessly uncomfortable, and psychologically harmful. There is little improvement due to fear of failure and even less in the way of learning and development due to chronic stress resulting from unrealistic expectations of continuously high personal and process performance. It is an ugly design that causes people to labor much more than necessary to get things done. Yet, the aesthetic judgment typically made by worker and CEO alike is: "It could be worse. There isn't anything better" [7]. But just because humans can adapt to an ugly design that results in ugly aesthetic experiences does not mean the design should not undergo a full redesign when needs dictate [8].

Of course, classical management exists in a multitude of similar forms, and many people who have worked within that design will say they had nothing but great experiences over the span of their careers. But data on employee engagement shows that nearly two-thirds of employees are not engaged or actively disengaged [9]. The Great Resignation of 2021-2022 is evidence of widespread employee dissatisfaction across all industry sectors. We can continue as-is, bearing whatever consequences occur over time and apply superficial fixes as usual. But, as we all claim to know, it is better correct problems immediately, at their root, so they do not grow into worse problems. Yet, the Institution of Leadership and the associated System of Profound Privilege [10-12], so very long in existence, are highly effective deterrents to redesigning classical management. Being calcified and maladaptive to changing conditions, the aesthetic compass rigidly points towards classical management as beautiful, with leaders' actions and inactions amply in accord with retaining and extending that highly valued aesthetic.

Yet we cannot allow the object, classical management, to force people conform to it. Instead, we must create a design where the object conforms to human needs, challenges and aspirations. We must then contemplate redesign of the aesthetically ugly object that we experience in organizations. Figure 3-2 shows a dodecahedron that we will use to represent progressive management. The prominent features of this design are roundedness, many surfaces, fewer sharp angles, and a smaller, less stable pentagonal base. Rounded features are generally considered more beautiful than sharp features, evoking the less angular, more curved Art Deco style of architectural design.

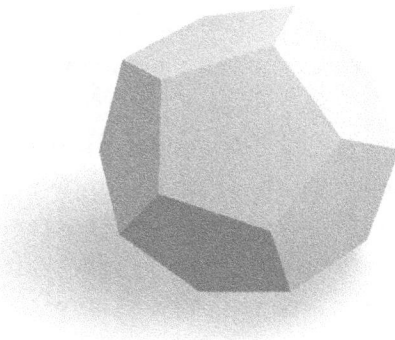

Figure 3-2. Object representing progressive management.

Think for a moment about management design. What should

be its major qualities and characteristics? A design is good and right if it serves a human purpose in ways that are both most beneficial and least destructive to all those who experience it, not just for a selected few, and least destructive to the environment – externalities that are fewer in number and severity (Figure 3-3). The design must therefore be responsive to the well-being of people and the larger living surroundings. It must have care and concern for human physical and mental health, as well as the health and well-being of the earth. It must be "green" in the context of being less toxic to all stakeholders than classical management. Curiosity and caring are seen as virtues, as well as recognizing and responding to human sensory perceptions of discomfort, discord, and deterioration.

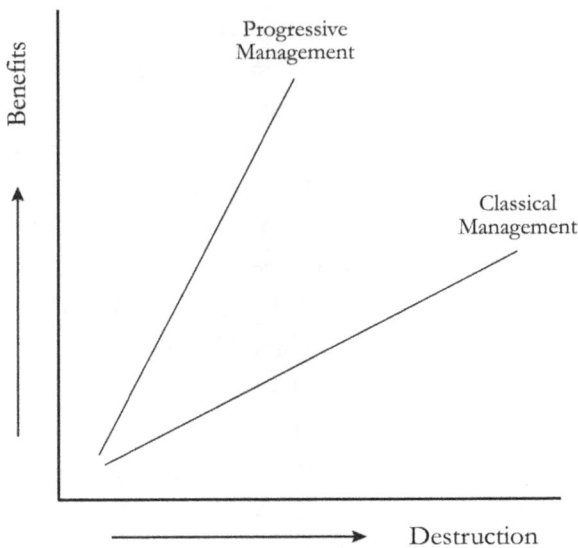

Figure 3-3. Benefits to humanity and destruction of humanity for classical management and progressive management.

The design would be bounded by respect for people *and* things, rather than careless disregard and disrespect for both. The design would enable people to be sensitive to change so that they can react in ways that produce progress rather than stasis. The path dependence would be based on learning and improving, not on rights and privileges or edicts handed down from authority. The design would be self-directing in its function to improve people's aesthetic experience and update aesthetic judgements as needed. On the local scale of an organization, and perhaps as well as on the larger scale of society, the design would have people question the social, economic, political, historical, philosophical, educational, business, technological, cultural, spiritual, aesthetic, and legal preconceptions that retard progress and threaten existence.

The dodecahedron, being a markedly different design, suggests the elimination of the negative aesthetic experiences that are common to classical management. Unlike the tetrahedron, its shape suggests something less threatening and the ability to move (roll), to make progress, with less force. This makes possible the ability to love and cherish the new object, progressive management, so that people will take care of it and nurture it so that something ever-better is achieved as time passes. It would not view any person, department, or function as less than, as is the case with classical management where finance is a Heaven filled with beautiful fortune-telling saints and manufacturing is a Hell filled with ugly ignorant sinners. With a caring attitude, rather than a careless attitude, people focus on maintaining and improving every part of the organization every day, knowing that such work, while exceptionally gratifying, never ends.

The challenge for top leaders is immeasurable. Their instinct is to control and manipulate people, things, and events. Most fall under the illusion that they can do this perfectly and suffer no ill consequences. Ego, arrogance, and pomposity, existing in unhealthy proportions and are visible to anyone with open eyes and ears, form the sharp tip of the classical management tetrahedron. Humility, widely known to be essential for great leadership, is rarely found. The dodecahedron object representing progressive management has no sharp tip. It has been rounded off. That means progressive leaders accept the need to transcend their ego, arrogance, and pomposity, and loosen their emotional attachments to rights, privileges, power, and special relationships. Using their six senses, they develop sensitivities to perceive conditions as they are, not as they would like them to be. They show and demonstrate respect for people and things, avoiding the procedural errors made by constantly categorizing and valuing, so that others can grow and learn from them. Instead of controlling human nature, they are attuned to it and allow employees to think for themselves, rather than think for them.

There is a clear undercurrent of moral and ethical virtues in progressive management, in recognition of human needs and aspirations, that are largely barren in classical management. The general or situational absence of moral and ethical virtues is a type of dishonesty (stealing) by top leaders that is thrust upon others and tellingly reveals indifference to others – especially those lower in the hierarchy or stakeholders external to the organization. Leaders can have concern for those lower in the hierarchy or act whimsically towards them and external stakeholders. The latter reflects an us-versus-them worldview, a form of battle, one that leads to crude stereotypes and varied forms of management malpractice. This is a manifestation of the destruction that classical management produces while it labors to produce its benefits to humanity.

Instead, one can lead and manage in ways that enhance the inherent appeal of work, organization, and purpose. Respect for people, respect for humanity, respect for nature, respect for materials, respect for non-art objects (pen, desk, stapler, or computer), respect for process, respect for the building – their animate and inanimate character. A shift in viewpoint from me to them, from subject to object, rooted in the aesthetic appreciation of human capabilities and creative potential, and a purging of the mentality that constructs in-groups and out-groups. Understanding non-art objects as precious things designed by, made by, and made for humans, by hand or by machine, also designed and made by humans.

Leaders can recognize that facts and problems presented to them are not something that is out of place, but is instead a most beautiful aesthetic, while telling the boss what they want to hear is the ugliest aesthetic of all. In classical management, unfavorable metrics and KPIs are taken as a personal affront to one's leadership abilities, an ugly aesthetic that initiates relentless blame. These are not cause for blaming people, but instead they are cause for helping people so that they can succeed. Blaming people for problems feels to be the natural thing to do, and thus beautiful, but progressive leaders understand it to be ugly and unnatural in both the act and its consequences. They understand it to nullify or greatly diminish the human creativity, energy, and spirit of the endless improvements needed for human survival.

Management design is a function of both people and processes. In classical management, both are in disarray. That might not be apparent if one is a participant in it or observing it from afar, but from the viewpoint of progressive management the perpetual disorder and messiness are unnatural and ugly: nasty organizational politics, departments fighting, conflicting metrics and KPIs, recurring problems, low morale, and dissatisfied customers. Glossy PowerPoint presentations may be perceived as objects of beauty, but what lurks below the surface is the kind of resource-absorbing messiness where problems multiply. Hence the need to give people at all levels the freedom to improve processes in ways that classical management severely restricts.

When people are allowed to think and be creative, they develop various methods to improve processes such that the time from start to completion is reduced, while assuring the work is simplified and easier to do so that people do not struggle. Subsequently, engaged employees think of creative ideas to further improve both the methods and processes. The resulting improvements in employee engagement, quality, cost, productivity, and employee satisfaction are indicative of greater order and predictability – characteristics highly sought after in classical management, but never attainable. People get used to the ugly chaos and stagnation and consider it normal. They cannot envision experiencing a beautiful stable and improving work environment (Figure 3-

4) because leaders will not allow it and employees lack the training to achieve it.

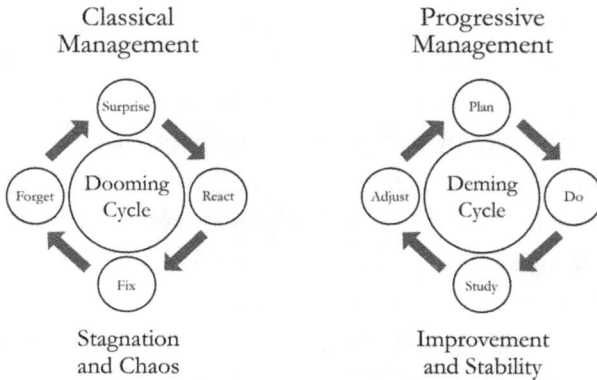

Classical
Management

Surprise

Forget | Dooming Cycle | React

Fix

Stagnation
and Chaos

Progressive
Management

Plan

Adjust | Deming Cycle | Do

Study

Improvement
and Stability

Figure 3-4. Process of stagnation and chaos in classical management and process of improvement and stability in progressive management.

It should be easy to understand that much like the design (blueprint and specification) of a product or service affects all downstream processes, the design of the management system impacts all people and processes in the organization. It shapes their aesthetic experience in ways that are ugly or beautiful. Fundamentally, progressive management is designed to be an evolving system such that people are happier in their jobs and overall work experiences. They are trusted by top leaders and authorized to think scientifically as they autonomously identify and correct problems in their work, the work of the team, or elsewhere. They have a measure of control over their work which, unlike chaotic and confusing classical management, reduces daily physical and mental stress.

The design of management systems, both the object and the resulting environment actualized by leaders, profoundly affect human experience. It is a powerful determinant to how people think, how they feel, how they act and interact, and how they live both at work and at home. The aesthetic experience of existing within organizations pervades all our senses: sight, sound, touch, smell, taste, and gut (emotion). Whether intended or not, management systems embody moral values – the beliefs, behaviors, habits, and practices, that are validated by the social environment people work in as informed by leaders' thinking and actions (Table 3-1).

Table 3-1   Moral Values in Management System Design

Positive Aesthetics	Negative Aesthetics
Respect	Disrespect
Caring	Uncaring
Sensitivity	Detachment
Empathy	Indifference
Awareness	Neglect
Appreciation	Disparagement
Gratitude	Ingratitude
Harmony	Discord
Intelligence	Ignorance
Humility	Arrogance
Wisdom	Ineptitude
Modesty	Vanity
Responsibility	Privilege
Kindness	Hostility
Diligence	Idleness
Fairness	Dishonesty
Duty	Irresponsibility
Logical	Irrational
Generous	Rapacious
Consideration	Disregard (for others)
Workmanship	Drudgery
Collaboration	Competition

These and other characterizations of moral values can easily be understood as features of good or bad management system design, whether consciously designed into the system or emergent from the system's day-to-day operation. Were one to redesign a management system, it would make no sense for the redesign to produce less benefit for humanity and greater destruction of humanity – as would allowing classical management to continue in the beautiful direction set by the aesthetic compass. Instead, any redesign should be thoughtful and considerate in terms of those who experience it, either *a priori* or *a posteriori*. Thoughtful design and thoughtful, real-time, correction of deficiencies in the redesign, would reveal a positive aesthetic of caring for people, processes, and outcomes.

Given the uniquely human character and intent of management systems, any design should have as its goals a humane system, one that results in positive aesthetic experiences, and which assists in developing people to their fullest capabilities. The emotive state is one that energizes and produces feelings of satisfaction, happiness, and other such qualities to enable people in the organization to do their best work. Classical management, having many negative aesthetic moral values, is an inconsiderate design due to its propensity to produce negative human sensory experiences for most who experience it. It can be more closely associated with art, rather than design, because it has fewer restrictions.

This aligns with the common view that leadership is an art. To think of leadership as being subject to causality would be to place abhorrent restrictions on leadership thinking and practice. It would force leaders to be more thoughtful and considerate, which in classical management stand as violations of leaders' rights and privileges and a diminution of power and honor. This generally assures that rank-and-file employees' sensory experiences will fall below their expectations day after day and year after year. From top leaders' perspective, the origin of negative aesthetics (Table 3-1) is the poor work done by both lower-level managers and workers. Ugly unfavorable performance metrics and KPIs and varied forms of bad news are a disgusting personal indignity to one's leadership and management acumen; a sign of carelessness and disrespect, and of defacing and degrading the company and its top leaders. Employees or departments are blamed for committing ugly aesthetic offenses that despoil the leader's view of self and company. Hence their general distrust of non-executive employees.

Such leadership behavior is thoughtless and inconsiderate, particularly given that process problems lie at the root of problems that leaders perceive as being caused by people. Blaming people for problems and similar psychopathic behaviors [13] such as public humiliation, manipulating people, taking credit for other people's work, intentional deceit, sabotaging other people or departments, etc., are antisocial and generates, rather than alleviates, human suffering, under the mistaken belief that suffering (e.g., workplace bullying) brings out the best in people [14]. Classical management is generally insensitive and unresponsive to most human needs. Those who have physical or mental disabilities are referred to as "special needs" people. The words are apt because their needs are indeed special. Yet human beings, as a species also have a type of need – certainly not equivalent to those with special needs – but similar in the narrower sense that their mental and physical health functions is impaired by inconsiderate thought and actions taken by others. The psychological, multi-sensory bodily experience that results in harm to employees is particularly bad when the source of predatory behavior is those at the top of the hierarchy [15].

Organizations committed to classical management often recognize such problems, but the actions typically taken are palliative, not prophylactic. This is to be expected given the general lack of interest in causality that exists in classical management. Proper root cause analysis would show that leaders need to change their thinking and behavior from negative to positive aesthetics (Table 3-1), which, once again, is an ugly violation of leaders' rights and privileges and a diminution of power and honor. The only way out of this situation is management system redesign which embodies the positive aesthetics of progressive management.

Most leaders treat the job of leadership and management as a simple design problem best solved through their aesthetic judgments, but which create negative experiences for others. The near-universal desire to simplify the problem in this way is because the problem is complex. Being at the top of the hierarchy bestows leaders with the right to solve the problem of leadership and management in ways that are most beneficial to them despite any ill consequences borne by others. This arrogant, narcissistic design alienates others who hope to contribute to the success of the organization and likely violates, in some measure, an organizations' code of ethics. A design focused on power and domination has the appearance of being sustainable, but it produces so many difficult problems that it will eventually topple the leadership or the organization.

The disregard or lack of attentiveness for care of oneself, other employees, and the organization spans generations of leaders, each thinking that the worst will never happen to them. Every day, business periodicals such as *The Wall Street Journal* and *Financial Times* document troubled or fallen leaders, yet the cause of their demise seems immaterial to their brethren. This produces a fertile ground for unknowingly repeating the mistakes made by other leaders. Yet one's status prevents most leaders from comprehending what is plainly visible to others, and who likely must remain silent for fear of upsetting the boss. It is widely cited that top leaders are avid learners, curious to learn new ideas and gain new insights. But if that were true, then most leaders would long ago have made the transition from classical management to progressive management.

Recall that the purpose of this book is to show how aesthetics may be an Occam's razor form of simple explanation for the static ways in which hierarchical organizations are led and managed by generations of leaders. Yet, the forgoing has described a complex situation, largely resulting from scores of social, economic, political, historical, philosophical, educational, business, technological, cultural, spiritual, aesthetic, and legal preconceptions. The two seem to be at odds, but they are not. Take, for example, Albert Einstein's formula for the equivalence of mass and energy: $E = mc^2$. It is a simple mathematical formula derived from complex sets of equations concerning the relationship between space and time ("special relativity"). Einstein's formula is an Occam's razor; a simple explanation for complex phenomena. While aesthetics is presented here as a simpler theory to explain a phenomenon whose underlying workings are complex [10-12], it is worthwhile to briefly explore this complexity by returning to the objects selected to represent classical management and progressive management: the tetrahedron and the dodecahedron. Figures 3-1 and 3-2 represented these as plain solid shapes. To explore the underlying complexity of aesthetics, we shall consider these two shapes as Rubik's three-dimensional puzzles, with the puzzles serving as metaphors for our design problems. Figure 3-5 shows a pyraminx, a tetrahedral puzzle containing four faces, with

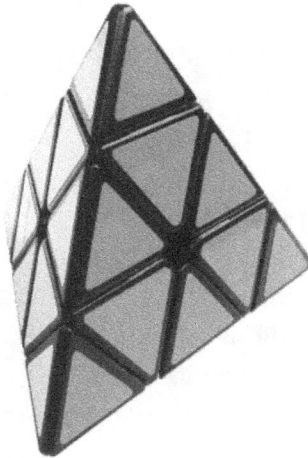

Figure 3-5. Pyraminx tetrahedral puzzle in the solved state (one color on each face).

each face a different color: red, blue, green, and yellow [16].

For our purposes, assume the volume of the pyraminx represents the problem space of classical management. For an edge length of 1, the volume is 0.118. The problem space of classical management, being small, reflects the fact that leaders who accede to classical management recognize and respond to only certain types of problems and ignore all others. The problem-space is bounded by preconceptions. Replace the color on each face of the pyraminx with one category of preconceptions such that four faces combined substantially (but not completely) describe the human character and intent of classical management [17-18]. The four categories of preconceptions are economic (pecuniary), social (status), political (relations among groups), and historical (path dependence). Each face of the pyraminx has nine colored triangles, each one representing a specific preconception [19]. Four categories of preconceptions times nine preconception per face equals 36 preconceptions.

Next, imagine the pyraminx puzzle all scrambled up. This represents a disordered state for the 36 preconceptions which must be ordered to solve the problems that exists in the pyraminx (classical management) problem space. There are 75,582,720 possible positions, reduced to 933,120 possible positions if rotating the tips is disregarded. It seems as if problem-solving should be complex, yet the preconceptions (categories and colors), unchanged for hundreds of years or more, greatly simplify problem-solving. The pyraminx is among the easiest three-dimensional puzzles to solve. It can be solved – one color on each of the four faces – in under one second. Likewise, some big problems in classical management can be "solved" very quickly, in less than one second, but quick solutions are often very bad solutions – such as blaming people for problems. This recalls the mere half-dozen "levers" that leaders often say they employ to achieve results.

The problems that exist in the problem space will change, but the solution space is limited by the same static set of 36 preconceptions. The result is a near-immovable cognitive bias of the form, "If all you have is a hammer, everything looks like a nail" [20]. Meaning, overreliance on that which is familiar, handed down from prior generations of leaders: the four categories of preconceptions and the 36 preconceptions. These preconceptions have as their main feature negative (Table 3-1), self-regarding aesthetics, operating under the simplistic and unrealistic design assumption that what is good for the leader is good, or good enough, for everyone. Yet in reality, the aesthetic experience for leaders is beautiful while the aesthetic experience for most others is ugly.

What about progressive management? Figure 3-6 shows a megaminx, a dodecahedral puzzle containing 12 faces, with each face a different color: dark blue, white, red, pink, green, yellow, ivory, green, gray, orange, purple, and light blue [21]. Assume the volume of the megaminx represents the problem space of progressive management. For an edge length of 1, the volume is 7.663. The problem space of progressive management is 65 times larger than the pyraminx, reflecting the fact that leaders who subscribe to progressive management recognize and respond to a much larger set of problems. The problem-space is also bounded by preconceptions, but ones that are not identical to those found in classical management. That is because the very nature of progressive management is to break the many preconceptions that hinder progress and form new preconceptions that enable progress.

Figure 3-6. Megaminx dodecahedral puzzle in the solved state (one color on each face).

Replace the color on each face of the megaminx with one category of preconceptions that combined substantially describe the human character and intent of progressive management. The twelve categories of preconceptions are social, economic, political, historical, philosophical, educational, business, technological, cultural, spiritual, aesthetic, and legal. Each face of the megaminx has eleven colored shapes, each one representing a specific preconception [17]. Twelve categories of preconceptions times ten preconception per face equals 132 preconceptions.

Next, imagine the megaminx puzzle all scrambled up. This represents a disordered state for the 132 preconceptions which must be ordered to solve the problems that exists in the megaminx (progressive management) problem space. There are 1.01×10^{68} possible positions. It seems as if problem-solving is impossibly complex, yet the megaminx puzzle can be solved – same 12 colors on each of the 12 faces – in under 30 seconds. So, big problems in progressive management can also be solved rather quickly. The problems that exist in the problem space will change, but the solution space is informed by the larger set of 132 preconceptions that change or evolve over time as needs dictate.

The result is avoidance of cognitive biases due to more detailed analysis of problems, deeper understanding of relationships between phenomena, and more creative problem-solving. Progressive management is much less reliant on that which is familiar, handed down from prior generations of leaders. These preconceptions have as their main feature positive (Table 3-1), other-regarding aesthetics. It operates under the realistic design assumption that aesthetic experiences and resulting aesthetic judgments must be beautiful, but in a different way – one that is prosocial and respects and cares for the interests of all stakeholders (people, processes, and outcomes), not solely leaders' interests, as times change.

Progressive management seeks to be responsive to the reality of those with whom it engages – employees, suppliers, customers, investors, and communities – with a conscious, thoughtful, sensitive regard for their varied interests. It is not perfect, and mistakes are made, yet learning is more efficient and effective due to continuous updating of thinking and methods. The goal of its design is to apply human imagination and creativity to understanding how aesthetic experiences unfold and whether the experience will be favorable to employees needs as well as the needs of the organization and its other stakeholders. It sees great virtue in simplicity, but not in the simplistic thinking of classical management. Progressive management challenges people to find Occam's razor-type solutions to difficult problems, rather than ignore difficult problems or put band-aids on them as is characteristic of classical management. It recognizes William of Occam's words from his book *Summa Logicae*, "It is futile to do with more what can be done with fewer" [22]. And so, there are carefully crafted principles, concepts, methods, and tools to avoid doing with more what can be done with less. This is a lesson in economy, connected to moral values and an ethic of care, that does not exist in classical management [23].

Aesthetic experiences and aesthetic judgments resulting from the realization of Occam's words – "It is futile to do with more what can be done with fewer" – are a type of beauty that is entirely different than the understanding of beauty in classical management Figure 3-7). The aesthetic compass for progressive management also points north, but it is of a completely different character. Where classical management ignores whatever is ugly or dull, progressive management confronts whatever is ugly or dull and sees it not just as an opportunity for improvement, but as a requirement that improvement take place quickly. Negative aesthetics are not seen as an affront to leadership or management, but as a natural consequence of existence. They catalyze people's curiosity to learn more about the problem and find elegant solutions that point toward beauty. Its preconceptions define the need for evolution, in contrast to classical management whose preconceptions define the need for equilibrium. The design of progressive management is clearly aligned with reality, while the design of classical management is a combination of make-believe and reality [24].

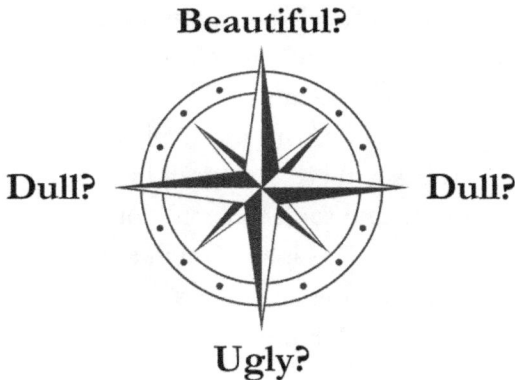

Beautiful?

Dull?   **Dull?**

Ugly?

Figure 3-7. Progressive management aesthetic compass also points in the direction of beauty, but a different kind of beauty. The question marks denote uncertainty and therefore the need to always question everything, especially whatever is judged to be beautiful, to be adaptive to changing times [25-26].

A management design that is better aligned with reality means to use the six human senses differently than how leaders use them in classical management, where sight, sound, and gut are central to executive thinking and decision-making. Touch – getting one's hands dirty – is the least useful sense because it lowers one's status to the level of workers. It impinges on leaders' rights and privileges and degrades one's honor and dignity. Getting one's hands dirty, experiencing what workers experience, is taboo. In progressive management, there is no such prohibition. In fact, it is unacceptable to not get one's hands dirty. Furthermore, the requirement to be a skilled observer means that leaders are far more highly attuned to sight, sound, and smell (Figure 3-8). Leadership and management practice better aligned with reality requires a reordering of sense priorities, something that is acquired by a social learning process that is fundamentally different than that found in classical management.

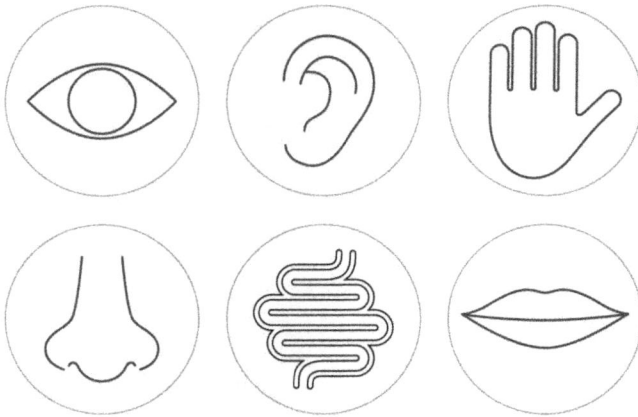

Figure 3-8. Six human senses. The top row – sight, sound, and touch (getting one's hands dirty) – are central to executive thinking and decision-making. Taste is the least useful sense for progressive leaders. Compare with Figure I-1.

"Everything is designed. Few things are designed well."
- Brian Reed

Ideas for Improvement

List some ideas to improve aesthetic experiences for employees and other stakeholders. Try out your ideas.

-

-

-

-

-

-

Notes

[1] Some of these fall into the category of fads, others are true innovations and may become mislabeled as fads.

[2] Predominantly men, of course, but women too.

[3] Dowd, D. (1958), *Thorstein Veblen*, Cornell University Press, Ithaca, New York, p. 157

[4] Emiliani, B. and Torinesi, M. (2021), *Wheel of Fortune: Getting to the Heart of Business Strategy*, Cubic LLC, South Kingstown, Rhode Island

[5] When someone makes a mistake, it is usually accidental but there is awareness that it was wrong. When one makes an error, it is an unintended deviation, meaning the person did not know. In the management of organizations, leaders sometimes claim to have made errors but not mistakes, thus avoiding culpability. More commonly, leaders refuse to admit both mistakes and errors.

[6] Emiliani, B. (2015), *Speed Leadership: A New Way to Lead for Rapidly Changing Times*, The CLBM, LLC Wethersfield, Connecticut

[7] Saying or thinking "It could be worse. There isn't anything better" serves as a justification for asking people to endure ugly aesthetic experiences and to conform to the prevailing social aesthetic judgment. From this follows the familiar phrase, "Be happy you have a job." Asking people to endure

hardship and struggle, to sacrifice themselves, is neither beauty nor virtue. The effect is to enforce a type of corporate patriotism that leaders see as being very useful but in fact diminishes the independent thinking internally and viewpoints external to the organizations that are necessary to survive and prosper. See Note 4.

[8] A full redesign does not mean completely scrapping 100 percent of classical management, as there are elements that may need to survive. One example is organizational hierarchy but modified in ways that discard the ugly features common in classical management and replaced with features that produce beautiful aesthetic experiences for both leaders and followers (and thus creates a new path). Human intelligence, plus awareness of cause-and effect, must be applied in any redesign, as well as rapid comprehension of problems post-redesign followed by quick improvement.

[9] Gallup (2022), "State of the Global Workplace" https://www.gallup.com/workplace/349484/state-of-the-global-workplace.aspx, accessed 8 March 2022

[10] Emiliani, B. (2018), *The Triumph of Classical Management Over Lean Management: How Tradition Prevails and What to Do About It*, Cubic LLC, South Kingstown, Rhode Island

[11] Emiliani, B. (2020), *Irrational Institutions: Business, Its Leaders, and The Lean Movement*, Cubic LLC, South Kingstown, Rhode Island

[12] Emiliani, B. (2020), *Management Mysterium: The Quest for Progress*, Cubic LLC, South Kingstown, Rhode Island

[13] See Babiak, P. and Hare, R. (2007), *Snakes in Suits: When Psychopaths Go to Work*, Harper Business, New York, New York, and https://en.wikipedia.org/wiki/Psychopathy_in_the_workplace, accessed 11 March 2022

[14] Of course, there is evidence now and then that a superior's psychopathic behaviors raise a subordinate's performance to new heights. Such examples succeed at confirming one's biases, which in turn leads to a perpetuation of negative aesthetics. The mountain of information disconfirming the effectiveness of antisocial behaviors is conveniently ignored.

[15] Psychological harm can also be inflicted by subordinates, peers, and managers below the executive level.

[16] See https://en.wikipedia.org/wiki/Pyraminx, accessed 13 March 20022

[17] Previous work (see Notes 10-12) described classical management as being informed by eight categories of preconceptions: economic, social, political historical, philosophical, business, spiritual and legal, with numerous preconceptions per category. The pyraminx is a simplified example focused on four preconceptions – economic, social, political historical. The present work identifies 12 categories of preconceptions: social, economic, political, historical, philosophical, educational, business, technological, cultural,

spiritual, aesthetic, and legal preconceptions, with some 10-12 preconceptions per category. These categories exist in both classical and progressive management, but most of the preconceptions are dissimilar.

[18] It might be helpful to think of preconceptions as a type of surface tension of liquids, akin to a stretched elastic membrane. The "surface tension" of classical management's preconceptions is strong, like liquid mercury, and thus thick and difficult to puncture and change. The "surface tension" of progressive management's preconceptions is weak, like water (5.8 times less than liquid mercury), and thus thin and easier to puncture and change or update when needed. The reduced "surface tension" of progressive management preconceptions helps avoid overreliance on that which is familiar. The analogy can be extended to capillary action (wicking effect). "Capillary action" is negative in the case of liquid mercury (convex and falling) – i.e., overreliance on that which is familiar resulting in the status quo. "Capillary action" is positive in the case of water (concave and rising) – i.e., curiosity about that which is unfamiliar resulting in evolution.

[19] A useful exercise for readers is to deduce, based on experience, nine preconceptions for each of the four categories of preconceptions: economic, social, political, and historical.

[20] See https://en.wikipedia.org/wiki/Law_of_the_instrument, accessed 13 March 20022

[21] See https://en.wikipedia.org/wiki/Megaminx, accessed 13 March 2022

[22] See http://www.logicmuseum.com/wiki/Authors/Ock ham/Summa_Logicae, accessed 14 March 2022

[23] In antiquity, pyramids are a tomb for the dead. In classical management, the pyramid is also a tomb, but for the living. Credit: Massimo Torinesi, 14 March 2022. And pyramids entomb more than bodies, but eventually societies as well. See Cooney, K. (2021), *The Good Kings: Absolute Power in Ancient Egypt and the Modern World*, National Geographic, Washington, D.C.

[24] The primary leverage points in the design of classical management that leaders use most are substantially make-believe.

[25] The question marks prompt people to ask: Why is it beautiful? What is the cause? What can be done to make it more beautiful? Why is it dull? What is the cause? What can be done to make it beautiful? Why is it ugly? What is the cause? What can be done to make it beautiful? The purpose of doing this is to instill in all employees, executives and non-executives alike, the capability to question assumptions and thus identify that which hinders progress. In doing so, the progressive management system evolves as do the products and services purchased by customers. This helps assure the organization keeps up with changing times and circumstances. Compare to the aesthetic compass for classical management shown in Figure 1-3.

[26] Much the same as when leaders seek new hires with good teamwork skills but instead tells them to do as they are told, leaders seek creative and innovative people and instead routinely dismiss their ideas. In these two examples, leaders say one thing and do another. This exposes both a deep inner dread of change (i.e., novel ideas and new methods) and a warm, welcoming attitude for the status quo. It is not a case of hypocrisy. Rather, it reflects an unconscious bias against change due to uncertainty of results. The difficulty is when proven results from new ideas or methods are waved away merely to satisfy a personal predilection for mental and physical comfort. Other judgments of leaders' hypocrisy may also be due to unconscious bias against change or other deeply felt concern.

4

Path Dependence and Change

Occasionally, a curious president or CEO comes along, takes an interest in progressive management, enthusiastically absorbs all they can as quickly as they can through experiential and book learning. They soon leave classical management behind. A typical comment is: "We should have been doing this all along." They realize there are better ways of thinking and doing work, both individually and in teams. They understand the connections between William of Occam's words, "It is futile to do with more what can be done with fewer," moral (aesthetic) values, the ethic of care, and the daily production of business results. They have become outsiders by choice, and they enthusiastically promote progressive management to their leadership peers. There are few takers, yet they persist year after year struggling for a just cause. People like this are extremely rare.

The more typical situation is a weeding-out process to eliminate independent thinkers who have a progressive vision for leadership and management. It often begins as follows: People at lower levels of the organization somehow become familiar with progressive management. They become intrigued, learn more, and begin to experiment with it. They experience success and failure, but overall favorable results, which drives enthusiasm to learn and do more. The favorable results they achieve may lead to advancement to higher levels of the organization. But there comes a point in their career where good results are not enough.

When these people are considered for executive-level positions, they are usually removed from consideration. Those who are enthusiastic about progressive management generally press hard for major changes, and for such changes to be made quickly. The executive team notices an outlier who will not fit in with other leaders because they have no desire for major changes. If the person happens to be promoted to executive level, they will likely be the least influential member of the executive team yet saddled with the near-impossible task of making various changes that their peers don't support, care about, or understand [1]. Under such circumstances, their tenure in the position will not last long. They will either leave because they can't get much done or will be forced out because they are ineffective at getting things done in a system designed to act against them.

Progress that could be achieved to improve the human condition is thwarted, and so the status quo prevails. Leadership and management of the organization remains as it has long been. Encased by nearly impenetrable preconceptions, future choices will be based on past experiences and past choices thereby sustaining the aesthetic of classical management. This is path dependency [2-4]. For it to occur there must be a causal link between preceding and subsequent events. Once a path has been chosen – and in the case of classical management, the path was chosen centuries ago – it seems beneficial to subsequent agents to continue along the same path. Not doing so might incur unwanted risks or costs. As the path lengthens over time, it develops a longer history that becomes regarded as a set of traditions that must be honored and preserved. This places restrictions on the future choices that leaders make. Traditions, commonly seen as stabilizing, can be destabilizing when forcefully brought forward to the present.

Change becomes bounded by the path dependent framework. Classical management does change in both intentional and unintentional ways, but always with the result that reinforces its entrenched position. Path dependent thinking, norms, practices, routines, and decisions produce institutional lock-in that retards progress that needs to be made if one is to stay current with the times in relation to the changing needs of people, organizations, and society. Classical management is locked-in, while progressive management, despite evidence of superiority, is locked-out. The goal, conscious or not, is to preserve an aesthetic that is judged by leaders to have been beneficial in the past and is seen as remaining beneficial presently and into the future.

The lock-in of classical management means leaders are largely unconcerned about its specific weaknesses and indifferent to better alternatives that are more efficient, and which produce a better balance of outcomes. Any major change is foreclosed by the past (sunk costs), which most leaders will surely find it easiest to comply with [5]. It is the established formula for success. The expectation is that lock-in will produce the same or better results as in the past, all other things being equal. But all other things are not equal. Times change, people's needs change, and society changes. Path dependency is a convenient way for leaders to ignore such changes and avoid expending the resources that are needed to confront such changes. Those resources can be directed to other purposes, or wasted, to fit with long-established preconceptions and expectations among those with vested interests.

Leaders' preference for suboptimal path dependent routines and outcomes lead to stagnation and a propagation of errors that may seem inconsequential. But eventually many leaders will suffer from a pile-up of errors that result in crisis [6]. That might provide sufficient impetus to switch paths, but the more typical outcome is to switch leaders and continue along the classical management path. The so-called "burning platform" – meaning, an internal or external shock or major discontinuity that requires leader to confront change or risk death – is often cited as the prime motivation for switching paths. That does work in some cases, but it is not universally successful as is commonly believed. The relatively few cases of change to progressive management succeed more as confirmation biases of the effectiveness of the "burning platform" than as an actual driver of change. Furthermore, there are many viable off-ramps in classical management that permit survival which negates the need for switching to a new progressive management path [7].

Classical management has had a great 350+ year run. It has done many good things for billions of people and societies – analog societies – around the world. We are now well into a new digital age and society is changing in expected and unexpected ways. Leaders must respect that reality and undergo the difficult but necessary change. Many people think that generational change will produce path switching from classical management to progressive management. It has not done so in the past and likely will not do so in the future. Why? As described in Chapter 2, children develop socially inherited understandings of classical management and the associated scores of preconceptions. Today's new leaders have been further instilled with classical management preconceptions by the prior generation of leaders, the prior generation was instilled with preconceptions by an earlier generation of leaders, and so on. Twenty-somethings today are being instilled with classical management preconceptions by leaders who are 40 to 60 years old. So, even the youngest generations have been primed to carry on archaic ways of thinking and the traditions of the past. They do not realize they are traveling on a locked-in path dependent route whose guardrails are the preconceptions they grew up with as children, learned as new employees, and put into practice as young managers (Figure 4-1).

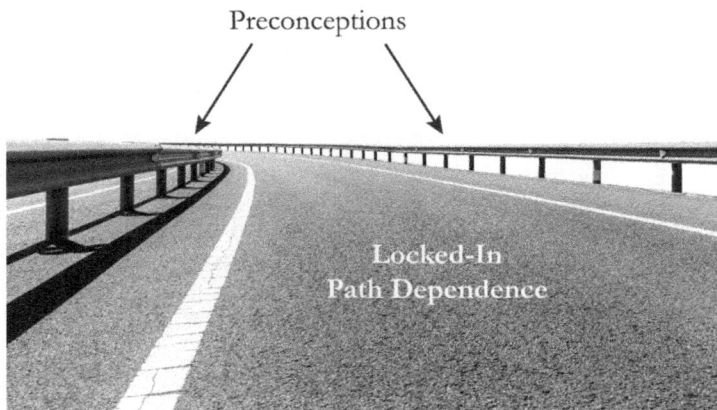

Figure 4-1. Preconceptions function as guard rails that lock-in classical management path dependence.

How does one break or switch management paths? There are a few ways:

- External shock
- Internal directive from the top leader
- Evolution
  - Personal: The rare, curious president or CEO who takes a great interest in progressive management.
  - Organizational: Experiential learning resulting from individual or team efforts to solve a big problem; many steps over some lengthy period of time.
- Combinations of the above

These are random occurrences wherein, for some reason, a firm conclusion is reached that the old management system must be replaced with a new management system. In reaching this conclusion, an inductively reasoned prediction is made that the progressive management offers near- and long-term benefits that exceed the expected benefits of continuing along with classical management. This initiates a contest between visions and challenges of the future and memories and habits of the past, one that affects all leaders as they struggle to abandon preconceptions that have seemingly served them so well in the past.

It is notable that progressive management has as its origins dissatisfaction with classical management. The people who created progressive management in its various forms knew classical management very well. The change was initiated by each one of these four ways listed above. While progressive management constitutes switching to a new path, it has roots in the old path. Avoiding progressive management is akin to denying one's ancestry, but with the added complications that leaders face: certain small losses of power, authority, rights, and privileges and potentially big losses in social status and honor among one's peer group. These are the rewards for being an outlier, which most leaders will not accept. They will predict, incorrectly, that certain small losses of power, authority, rights, and privileges will lead to much larger losses in the future. And they will inductively reason, perhaps somewhat correctly, that the potential loss of social status and honor among one's peers, as well as access and opportunity, is completely unacceptable. Most leaders are therefore unwilling to set a precedent and switch to a new path, despite the non-zero probability of being wrong.

That leaves few options for those who wish to advance progressive management. The major failing across generations of progressive management advocates has been its exclusivity and factionalism. Progressive management advocates see themselves as smarter and far more enlightened than everyone else, and so they prefer to self-segregate and interact with one another. In recent decades, there has been no substantive collaborative strategies or tactics put in place to widen the appeal of progressive management. There are individual efforts to engage more people, but the usual result is to merely speak to one's followers. As with most efforts to achieve meaningful change, the group splits up into factions, each with a different understanding and practice of progressive management, ranging from ultra-low fidelity to ultra-high fidelity. This sows confusion within and outside the community of progressive management practitioners. Progressive management will not proliferate if it remains the province of a small group of forward-thinking people who are not aligned.

The obverse of this failure has been the unwillingness of progressive management advocates to look outward and engage, in substantive ways, union and non-union workers and society at-large. To inform and educate them about progressive management, to compare and contrast progressive management with classical management, to honestly show and discuss progressive management successes and failures, to seek dialog and ideas for improvement that would make progressive management more appealing to much larger numbers of people – not just workers, hourly and salary, but everyone, to make common the knowledge there are better ways of leading and managing organizations that produce better outcomes for all stakeholders. These inward and outward failures reveal progressive management's own path dependence problems; an inertia resulting from preconceptions that prevents path-switching away from exclusivity and factionalism.

In academia, business, leadership, and management are categorized as social sciences. As such, solutions to social problems – poor leadership and management resulting from outdated classical management – lay primarily in the social sciences. What, then, are the methods used to change public opinion and produce social change that better reflects the interests and needs of those who work for a living and society? It usually involves forcing change through peaceful means, and follows this general pattern:

- Grass roots organizing
- Unite with other organizations working to achieve different but complementary ends
- Don't position things in ways that creates losers or requires them to give up something (avoid zero-sum outcomes)
- Focus on those who can pressure leaders for change (in politics it is voters, in organizations it is workers)
- Develop novel legal theories to mount challenges to the status quo
- Create an easily identifiable symbol that people can wear or display to show their support
- Use social media (opportunity to go viral), radio, and other platforms that reach large number of people
- Create many short, jarring videos or infomercials (honest and realistic, not utopian)
- Call upon celebrities for support
- Ask elected leaders to take a position
- Be open to learning from each other throughout the process of challenging the status quo

And realize that winning is only temporary, so don't stop working to bring about change because many leaders will want to return to the way things once were. Work collaboratively with all stakeholders and engage in joint problem-solving when difficulties arise. It is an open question as to whether today's advocates of progressive management have it within them to organize themselves in this way. Thus far, they have shown no interest in undertaking such a challenge, preferring instead to exist as self-interested actors under the guise of collective interest. An alternate approach is harm reduction: to reduce the harm to people and planet (inefficient consumption of resources, pollution, etc.) due to externalities generated by classical management. Harm to employees is caused by a variety of stressors in the workplace that force employees to experience chronically high stress and places the burden on them to find ways of coping. Stressors arise principally from the poor design of work processes, poor and inconsistent leadership communication and interactions, metrics and KPIs that drive improper and unhealthy behaviors, and the existence of psychopaths in management positions ranging from supervisor to CEO. Chaotic and confusing workplaces with ever-changing directives and unclear expectations induce feelings of never being in control of one's work, one's life at work, and even one's personal or home life given the vicissitudes of employment in the 21st century.

Rather than seeking the unattainable, a world in which most or all organizations are progressively managed, one can instead work to reduce the damage caused by classical management. The focus could be on making visible the many errors that leaders make in interacting with people, especially employees [8-9], which cause physical and mental distress, and the errors in leadership decision-making caused by untested beliefs and assumptions, illogical thinking, and cognitive biases [6] which destabilize organizations. Harm reduction could be made the measure of success rather than path-switching.

The obvious difficulty with harm reduction is that over the past 100 years there have been myriad formulations to reduce the harm caused by classical management. The training and consulting industry is both contributor to and long-time beneficiary of the dysfunction caused by classical management's design. Their work is not without merit. Improvement is achieved for a while, sufficient to claim success, but soon there is a change in top leadership which causes a quick reversion to old ways of thinking and doing. The aesthetic of classical management prevails despite efforts to reduce the harms it causes.

The aesthetic experience of classical management is just too good for leaders. It is magnetic. And so aesthetic judgments strongly favor the preservation of classical management preconceptions and related thinking, practices, and appearances. Self-reinforcing feedback strengthens path dependence, both its technical outlook (e.g., investment in machinery, robots, automation, artificial intelligence, etc., to eliminate workers) and especially its social outlook (i.e., status, rights, privileges, honor). History matters because it produces a legacy of thinking and practices that generate inertia against change. This comes not just from leaders, but from half or more of the workforce because they are uncertain how change will affect them. Oftentimes, "change for the better" is oversold and has underdelivered, as long-time workers have learned from experience.

Another consideration is the structural inertia that comes from stakeholders. Organizations do not stand alone. They are part of a network of stakeholders and other interested parties, all of whom prefer the aesthetic of classical management. Take for example a large company with a corporate office and several separate business units. It is unlikely an individual business unit will be permitted to switch paths to progressive management because it changes leadership routines, management practices, the type of data collected and reports submitted, and executive interactions with the corporate office. A large classically managed company that buys a smaller progressively managed company will face new owners who will likely insist on doing things their way and force them to switch paths to classical management.

Companies engage with many suppliers, most of whom conduct business according to the strictures of classical management. It is impossible to disentangle from the network of classically managed organizations. Institutional investors, stock analysts, private equity groups, etc., are locked into classical management and view progressive management as an unnecessary distraction that yields little or no meaningful results. Leaders of all kinds are locked-in: private enterprise, government (political leaders and career bureaucrats), non-government organizations, religious, public safety, military, education, and so on. The perception of ever-increasing favorable returns and the illusion of control that come from being locked-in remains in effect [10].

The stability and persistence of the classical management aesthetic is remarkable. Unlocking its path dependence may be the singular challenge of our times to assure the survival of humanity. We can wait patiently, stuporously, for an external shock sometime in the future to propel needed change, or we can use human intelligence and wisdom to recognize that classical management no longer serves its original purpose, and that we are several decades late in recognizing that fact and must begin the process of switching paths.

• • • • • • • •

"A man who cannot think is not an educated man however many college degrees he may have acquired. Thinking is the hardest work any one can do – which is probably the reason why we have so few thinkers... If education consisted in warning the young student away from some of the false theories on which men have tried to build, so that he may be saved the loss of the time in finding out by bitter experience, its good would be unquestioned. An education which consists of signposts indicating the failure and the fallacies of the past doubtless would be very useful...the best that education can do for a man is to... teach him how to think."

- Henry Ford

Ideas for Improvement

List some ideas to improve aesthetic experiences for employees and other stakeholders. Try out your ideas.

-

-

-

-

-

-

Notes

[1] One common directive that top leaders give to the vice president is to (single-handedly) deliver "culture change" throughout the organization. Barring luck, failure is certain. Culture change is not the responsibility of a single individual. It is the responsibility of an aligned management team, consistent in their new thinking and practices.

[2] Sydow, J. (2021), "Path Dependence and Routine Dynamics" in D'Adderio, L., Dittrich, K., Feldman, M.S., Pentland, B.T., Rerup, C., & Seidl, D. (Eds.): *Cambridge Handbook of Routine Dynamics*, Cambridge University Press, Cambridge, UK, pp. 502-512

[3] Sydow, J., Schreyögg, G., and Koch, J. (2009), "Organizational Path Dependence: Opening the Black Box," *Academy of Management Review*, Vol. 34, No. 4, pp. 689-709

[4] Laudien, S.M., Daxböck, B. (2016) "Path Dependence as a Barrier to Business Model Change in Manufacturing Firms: Insights from a Multiple-Case Study." *Journal of Business Economics*, Vol. 86, pp. 611–645 https://doi.org/10.1007/s 11573-015-0793-1

[5] Some leaders allow the use of certain progressive management methods and tools to be used by lower-level employees to improve business efficiency. But they remain steadfastly against replacing the management system, classical management, with progressive management. Most leaders have no interest in being seen as an outlier among their peers

and suffer diminution of status and influence. They also want to avoid both the tedious work of having to learn a new system and uncertain outcomes. The idiom, "better the devil you know" reflects emotional and intellectual comfort with the existing path and great emotional and intellectual discomfort with any new path.

[6] Emiliani, B. and Torinesi, M. (2021), *Wheel of Fortune: Getting to the Heart of Business Strategy*, Cubic LLC, South Kingstown, Rhode Island

[7] See Table 1-2, page 34, in Emiliani, B. (2018), *The Triumph of Classical Management Over Lean Management: How Tradition Prevails and What to Do About It*, Cubic LLC, South Kingstown, Rhode Island

[8] Emiliani, B. (2015), *Speed Leadership: A New Way to Lead for Rapidly Changing Times*, The CLBM, LLC Wethersfield, Connecticut

[9] Goh, J., Pfeffer, J. and Zenios, S. (2015), "The Relationship Between Workplace Stressors and Mortality and Health Costs in the United States," *Management Science*, Vol. 62, No. 2, pp. 1-21, http://dx.doi.org/10.1287/mnsc.2 014.2115

[10] While leading an autocratic nation is dissimilar in many ways to leading an organization, this article, "Vladimir Putin Has Fallen Into the Dictator Trap," by Brian Klaas, highlights many of the common traps that leaders fall into which lock-in path dependence and make switching paths difficult.

See https://www.theatlantic.com/ideas/archive/2022/03/p
utin-dictator-trap-russia-ukraine/627064/,   accessed   16
March 2022. See also "Hubris and Isolation Led Vladimir
Putin to Misjudge Ukraine," by Paul Sonne, Ellen
Nakashima, Shane Harris and John Hudson, The
Washington Post, 11 April 2022, https://www.washington
post.com/national-security/2022/04/11/putin-misjudged-
ukraine-hubris-isolation/, accessed 12 April 2022. When
faced with an illness, patients smartly resign themselves to
doctors' expertise. Why? Neither Facebook nor Google nor
one's own intelligence makes then a physician. Top leaders,
however, often mistakenly assume they are the expert best
qualified to cure the ills of the organization (that being the
preferred aesthetic), thus ignoring the many real experts that
exist low in the hierarchy. This simple mistake has been made
by most leaders for thousands of years, to the continuing
detriment of humanity. The lack of learning from one's
predecessors, from one's peers, or from history, is
remarkable. Hence the real dangers to oneself and others that
come from status and privilege. The wise understand
leadership to be an error-prone activity, not an error-free
activity (see Note 8). They seek *and listen* to the counsel of
others no matter their rank.

Closing Comments

The Aesthetic Compass presents an Occam's razor explanation for the largely static way in which organizations have been led and managed by generations of leaders. This simpler theory explains a phenomenon whose underlying workings are complex. It shows the ways in which aesthetics powerfully inform top leaders' thinking and decision-making, resulting in action and inaction to preserve traditions and maintain the status quo with respect to leadership and management practice. There is no secret plan to do this. Instead, it is an informal alliance of leaders who share scores of preconceptions about leadership and management – some instilled as children, others as adults – combined with inductive thinking that seek to preserve and enhance their status, rights, privileges, power, authority, and special relationships [1-2]. Classical management is most efficient at achieving these "beautiful" ends and therefore remains the preferred system. A change in aesthetics is, in some measure, a conflict about two different sets of preconceptions.

Despite everyone's familiarity with management and the massive academic and trade literature on the topic, it is poorly understood and largely unexplored when it is framed as an aesthetic. Non-art aesthetic objects hide in plain sight, often overlooked by daily routines, but nevertheless profoundly affects people's experiences and results in judgments of what is beautiful and what is ugly. The aesthetics of classical management define a system whose design, function, and outcomes are markedly different than progressive management. The archaic nature of classical management is obvious in terms of its negative moral aesthetics and the ugly aesthetics experienced by most workers. Lionizing beauty is seen as a rational choice that must never be transgressed. This makes clear the need for progressive leadership and management that is current with the times, positive in its moral aesthetics, and produces beautiful aesthetic experiences for workers and others.

Yet, classical management preconceptions and aesthetic judgements of beauty, rooted in patriarchy, together result in path dependence that makes switching to a new path difficult. Classical management is locked-in by the past due to the perception of ever-increasing favorable returns and the illusion of control. The design of classical management is preferred because it results in aesthetics that best satisfy the emotional needs of leaders (i.e., status, rights, privileges, honor, etc.) – but not the emotional needs of others. This explains why "trust your gut" is widely considered as excellent advice to give to new leaders and commonly cited as a key leadership competency, with facts and reason being secondary or tertiary considerations. While leaders adjust the design of classical management in response to demands from employees (e.g., work from home or insurance coverage for mental health), self-reinforcing feedback strengthens path dependence assures that the result is status quo in leadership and management thinking and practice. Consequently, progressive management is locked-out, as is reason, which thwarts efforts to improve the human condition in organizations and in society.

This is not inconsequential. Aesthetic experience exists

because of bodily reaction to sensory stimuli [3]. This results in feelings of comfort (beauty) and discomfort (ugly), the latter of which may result in the initiation of inquiry as to the cause of discomfort. People begin to engage in efforts to determine the source of the discomfort, which could be psychological (anxiety, depression), physical (muscle ache, headache, stomach upset), or both. If others (subordinates, peers, or superiors) seem to not be in discomfort, then the most logical explanation is that the person experiencing discomfort is responsible for their own discomfort: "It must be my fault that I feel this way." This can manifest itself as chronic illness or employee turnover. Either way, it works to the advantage of top leaders because they are emancipated from having to change the way they lead and manage the organization to reduce bodily discomfort – the negative aesthetic experiences that exist in the workforce.

Given the long investment in classical management, leaders will likely put sustained effort into trying to maintain and fortify it and thus avoid switching paths to progressive management. Yet this is akin to raising the dead. This idea is flawed in both its conception and in the details for doing so. For example, classical management relies on the wisdom of a few (leaders), rather than many (leaders and workers). The design of classical management requires that leaders hear only good news, which means that information flows will become distorted or blocked, leaving leaders with an inaccurate view of reality. When bad news arises, the reactionary response is to blame others [4]. Dissent, usually, is not tolerated. Consequently, classical management attracts sycophants, as well as psychopaths, and succumbs to unhealthy leader (hero) worship. The notion of leaders being in service to others is scorned. Classical management has inherent weaknesses which limit the fullness of life experience that people desire. Time has passed and so must classical management. It should be heartily appreciated for what it has done in the past, as well as recognizing what it has failed to do. Hence, the need for change.

Younger generations have different wants and needs that go largely unfulfilled with classical management. They seek positive, prosocial aesthetic experiences in the workplace; respect, thoughtfulness, caring, and consideration – aesthetic experiences that only progressive management is designed to deliver [5]. Adherence to classical management disallows consideration of leadership and management innovations and inhibits change, adaptation, and evolution. Leaders are known for their fidelity to pragmatism and expediency but have yet to recognize it when it comes to progressive management. Evolution is a fundamental life process that no one is immune from participation, even if the aesthetic compass says otherwise. Leaders' aesthetics must change as the needs of others and as changing times dictate. The disorder, chaos, complexity, and strangeness that reflects the reality we live in is governed more effectively by progressive management. Leadership action and inaction should be of a nature that permits the establishment and steady evolution of progressive management [6].

Progressive management is a democratized vision [7] of leadership and management defined by facts and a mind less prone to interpret new aesthetic experiences in terms of past aesthetic experiences [8]. It uses human imagination and creativity to generate new knowledge, rather than using and reusing expired knowledge, and new reservoirs of wisdom. Progressive management aims for social unity (i.e., real teamwork) informed by a different conception of beauty and utility intertwined with life processes so that humans can thrive. Effectiveness is seen as more beautiful than the raw efficiency of classical management [9].

The negative moral aesthetics listed in Table 3-1 describe an aesthetic that is seen by leaders as beautiful because it produces the desired status, rights, privileges, power, authority, and special relationships. Beauty must instead be seen as that which is most beneficial to the growth and survival of humanity, not selected individuals. Progressive management aims for social interdependence and cooperative action in problem-solving rather than individuality. Sharing power in the limited forms embodied in progressive management produces a unifying sentiment that instills curiosity and invigorates people to think creatively of elegant ways to solve difficult problems. The resulting aesthetic experience is better attuned to what people desire and is more responsive to the fast-changing digital age we now live in (Figure C-1).

This volume has brought awareness of the important role of aesthetic experiences and aesthetic judgments in management systems. It has exposed classical management, born in the distant past, as not fit for current and future times. Classical management is irresponsible, insensitive, uncaring, neglectful, and likely immoral. It robs non-leaders of the

	Ugly	Beautiful
Classical Management	Workers Processes Shop/office floor Problems Logic Facts Change Unfavorable metrics Regulators Suppliers	Hierarchy Status and privilege Growth No problems Status quo Blaming people Glossy presentations Individual gain Do as you are told Obsequiousness
Progressive Management	Status quo Conflict Waste Neglect Organizational politics Conflicting metrics Recurring problems Dissatisfied customers Comfort Arrogance Disrespect	People Humanity Nature Facts Processes Problems Thinking Creativity Teamwork Learning Evolution

Figure C-1. Two-by-two matrix containing some of the aesthetics characteristic of classical and progressive management.

fullness of experience that they seek by coercing their participation in doing what is most aesthetically pleasing to leaders. It is not an exaggeration to say that given that classical management is outdated, leaders who continue with it impose their fantasy on others to continuing ill effect.

What is the way forward? Leaders must see themselves as designers responsible for creating the aesthetic experiences of other people. The future aesthetic must move away from classical management towards the direction of improvement exemplified by progressive management. There is no formula for doing that. But a first step for leaders is to learn the many aspects classical management and associated leadership thinking and practice that they likely are not even aware of. *The Aesthetic Compass* is the fourth and final volume in a series of books [10-12] that closely examined varied aspects of the traditional leadership and management design still in widespread use. Together, these four works provide ample direction for top leaders to design beautiful aesthetic experiences for others [13].

Finally, it is hoped that this volume has provided readers with the catalyst to rethink their understandings of leadership and management, to begin to leave behind archaic classical management, and to more effectively contend with the social pressure to continue conforming to archaic ways of thinking and doing things. Progressive management is not your enemy. It is your future [14-15]. And it is our future, given that technology alone will not solve all of humanity's problems.

"I am not saying that you have to discard all traditional ideas; I am only saying that you must not accept them as limitations. Most people either do not understand this or refuse to believe it. They are afraid of doing the exact opposite of what their predecessors have done and taught them to do… There are many things in this world you can't understand until you try them. With many things, you find the result is the exact opposite of what you expected."

- Taiichi Ohno

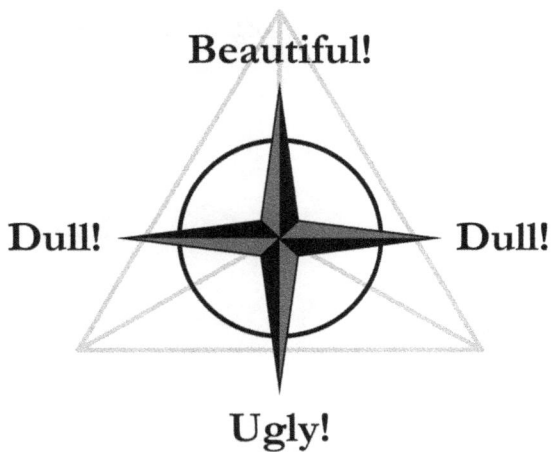

Beautiful!

Dull!   Dull!

Ugly!

- or -

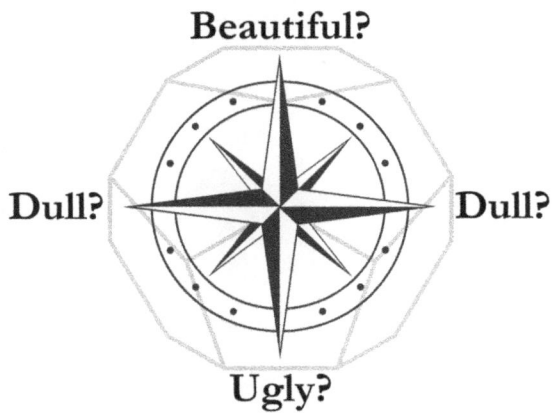

Beautiful?

Dull?   Dull?

Ugly?

Ideas for Improvement

List some ideas to improve aesthetic experiences for
employees and other stakeholders. Try out your ideas.

-

-

-

-

-

-

Notes

[1] This book has emphasized leader's interests in relation to status, rights, privileges, power, authority, and special relationships in their desire to perpetuate classical management. There is clearly a financial benefit that leaders seek as well. However, this was not a point of focus because it introduces base motivations outside the realm of aesthetics in organizations. Additionally, leaders' remuneration is not an everyday aesthetic experience in the same way that non-art objects are. Finally, remuneration is not always directly connected to leaders' action and inaction in relation to the preservation of classical management. However, money does have the property of introducing biases that favor traditions.

[2] Generally, masculine individuals are more concerned about status, rights, privileges, power, authority, and special relationships – as well as risk-taking, overt confrontation, competition, force, domination, conflict, and retaliation to gain or sustain these – than feminine individuals. The latter's preference tends to be cooperative relationships, building alliances, fairness, care, preventing harm, sensitivity, harmony, etc. Feminine individuals handle threats differently than masculine individuals. That is not to say that feminine individuals don't care about status, rights, privileges, power, authority, and special relationships. Their senses generally interpret these things differently in relation to their preferences. No doubt one can find many examples where these characteristics are reversed. The masculine authoritarian is assuredly far less helpful to other people than the feminine empath, the latter obviously being much more

valuable in organizations and society than the former (i.e., propensity for problem-solving versus problem-making), suggesting both would be better off with majority feminine leaders – those who do not succumb to the banality of facile masculine dispositions and traditions. This is difficult to do given that anyone at the top of a hierarchy must contend with political and pecuniary concerns that often favor unimaginative masculine prescriptions and responses.

[3] Tschaepe, M. (2021), "Somaesthetics of Discomfort," *European Journal of Pragmatism and American Philosophy*, Vol. 13, No. 1, pp. 33-42

[4] Fear is an archaic conception of social control. Yet for most top leaders, what worked 5,000 or more years ago remains very useful to them today. Progressive management is a far less fear-based way to meet or exceed organizational objectives. Leaders don't need fear to triumph.

[5] Progressive management, being prosocial, is better for individuals and supports families. It does this by removing most of the stressors that pervade classical management which harms individuals and families. And it reduces volatility in employment which results in a steadier stream of income for the employee. The pro-family aspect of progressive management should not be underestimated and seen in relation to the severely and painfully anti-family nature of classical management.

[6] In progressive management, leadership action and inaction are directed towards avoiding complacency and not

reverting to classical management.

[7] A democratized vision of leadership and management is immediately suspect in the eyes of leaders. It is an almost instant disqualifier, as most leaders fear democracy in organizations even if it is carefully circumscribed as it is in progressive management. Glorifying business leads to political contempt for democratic values.

[8] Avoid falling into the trap of thinking of leadership, and management, as an art. If you do that, you will think as people did 100 years ago, and longer. Aesthetic experiences and aesthetic judgments are clearly the result of both preconceptions and causality. It is only by switching paths, from preconceptions to fact-based sensory perceptions (different causal relationship), that one can make the types and quantities of progress that are needed.

[9] Progressive management is not perfect. It has flaws. Its strength is in its fundamental design which compels people to improve and evolve the system as well as one's own thinking and practices as times and circumstances change. Classical management is highly prescriptive and static in its solutions for correcting problems. Progressive management offers new concepts, different ways of thinking, supports constant experimentation as the preferred method for problem-solving and adaptation. The resulting organizational learning accumulates at a much faster rate than classical management, and it results in a better work experience for employees and better business results.

[10] Emiliani, B. (2018), *The Triumph of Classical Management Over Lean Management: How Tradition Prevails and What to Do About It*, Cubic LLC, South Kingstown, Rhode Island

[11] Emiliani, B. (2020), *Irrational Institutions: Business, Its Leaders, and The Lean Movement*, Cubic LLC, South Kingstown, Rhode Island

[12] Emiliani, B. (2020), *Management Mysterium: The Quest for Progress*, Cubic LLC, South Kingstown, Rhode Island

[13] And think of colors in your new design. Replace the ugly drab brown color of everyday work experience with beautiful vibrant colors that excite and engage people, and which makes them happy. See the colors on front cover.

[14] Perhaps the only thing that stands between top leaders and progressive management is motivated reasoning, consciously or subconsciously – rejecting facts that are not consistent with one's identity as a leader and social and cultural affiliation with peer leaders. It is, or seems to be, an injurious (sociopathic) use of one's emotional and intellectual capacities. After all, leaders exist in the short run, while organizations and societies exist in the long run. The view of leadership and management is organized around the foundational ideas that authority and privilege must never be abridged. This provides ample motivation for leaders to reason the sanctity of classical management and its continuation, and to extinguish rightful desires for that which is better. And this, in turn, makes self-evident the need for fact-based progressive management.

[15] Classical management and progressive management can be thought of as a conflict over traditions (as well as associated preconceptions). Traditions, fundamentally, are deeply held aesthetics. It is a clash between preserving long established aesthetics – those relevant to both classical management and progressive management, some of which are shared – abandoning certain aesthetics, and constructing new aesthetics. For example, see Note 5.

About the Author

M.L. "Bob" Emiliani is a professor in the School of Engineering, Science, and Technology at Connecticut State University in New Britain, Conn., where he teaches a course on leadership, a unique course that analyzes failures in management decision-making, as well as other courses.

Bob earned a Bachelor of Science degree in mechanical engineering from the University of Miami, a Master of Science degree in chemical engineering from the University of Rhode Island, and a Doctor of Philosophy degree in engineering from Brown University.

He worked in the consumer products and aerospace industries for 15 years, beginning as a materials engineer. He has held management positions in engineering, manufacturing, and supply chain management at Pratt & Whitney.

Bob joined academia in September 1999. While in academia, he developed a new teaching pedagogy and led activities to continuously improve master's degree programs.

Emiliani has authored or co-authored 25 books, four book chapters, and more than 45 peer-reviewed papers. He has received six awards for his writing.

Please visit www.bobemiliani.com